D1481713

The Quiet World of
STEVE
HOPKINS

To Marsh —

Many quiet moments —

Steve Hopkins

BY STEVE HOPKINS

Copyright© 1989 Steve Hopkins

Designer
Linda Brazill

Front Cover Photo by L. Roger Turner
Back Cover Photo by Chris Corsmeier

Published by William C. Robbins
and Straus Printing Company, Madison, Wisconsin

All rights reserved. No part of this publication may be reproduced or transmitted in any
form or by any means, electronic or mechanical, including photocopy, recording or any
information storage or retrieval system without permission in writing. For information
contact The Wisconsin State Journal, P.O. Box 8056, Madison WI 53708.

For Frances —
and for Peter, Katy and Jayne.

INTRODUCTION
1

Chapter One
AT THE CABIN
5

Chapter Two
FATHERS AND SONS
23

Chapter Three
CANOES, SNOWSHOES AND A CLIMB
35

Chapter Four
NOSTALGIA
47

Chapter Five
QUIET PEOPLE. QUIET PLACES.
69

Chapter Six
BUMMING AROUND
87

Chapter Seven
SIFTING AND WINNOWING
105

Chapter Eight
FIREPLACE DAYS
125

Chapter Nine
PAGES FROM THE CABIN JOURNAL
139

Chapter Ten
AND FINALLY
157

Waiting out a summer squall on the White River.

INTRODUCTION

People have asked, through the years, if there ever would be a collection of some of my scribblings — and I always have answered that maybe there would be, someday.

Somedays don't always arrive; more often than not they are elusive dreams, ghostly ships which loom on distant horizons, but, for some reason or other, never come in.

This one came in, but it took awhile to get here, 20 years or so. The pieces in this book were gleaned from almost 1,000 columns written during that same period of time.

There are not nearly that many in the book, but the ones I chose were some of those I liked the best and those which most faithfully reflect the things that interested me and the things I chose to record. They are, I think, pretty good samples of what my column has been about.

1

There are stories in here about the cabin — in 40 acres of Vernon County woods — and about the times my wife, Frances, and our children, Peter, Katy and Jayne, spent there.

There are stories about the changing of the seasons, the precision of which continues to fascinate me even into my advancing years.

There are stories about bumming around — on foot, on snowshoe and by canoe.

There are stories about some men, and women, I have known, and about some I wish I had known. There are stories about a boy growing up and, finally, going away.

If you remember railroads and steam locomotives and old cars and small towns the way they used to be, there is plenty of that in here, too. There is a little travel and there is just a touch of music.

I have tried to arrange these pieces by subject, but not necessarily in chronological order. Except for a few minor editing changes they appear here exactly as they appeared in the newspaper because to try to update them would alter and destroy their original character.

I will try to bring a few things up to date.

Peter grew up and graduated from the University of Alaska at Anchorage and now works for an accounting firm there. He and his wife, Gretchen, live in Anchorage.

Katy graduated from the University of Wisconsin-Whitewater and, as of this writing, is teaching second grade on the Navajo reservation at Shiprock, N.M. She is living in Farmington, N.M.

Jayne, the youngest, graduated from UW-Madison and lives with her recently acquired husband, Lee Kubler, in St. Paul, Minn. She is an early childhood educator with a social services agency.

Some of the oldtimers I have written about, all good friends who were kind enough to take a green youngster in hand and teach him some of the ropes of the outdoors, are no longer with us. I will be eternally grateful to them — and I miss them all.

I no longer smoke the pipe I sometimes refer to in these stories; it is a habit I gave up a few years ago. I haven't sported a beard for a couple of years now and probably never will again. That was a stage in my somewhat arrested development, I think, that I just kind of outgrew.

The cabin still plays a major role in our lives and Frances and I spend a few days there whenever we can. It still isn't quite finished and probably never will be. We like it that way.

I am most at home when I am there — and the Steve Hopkins who lives in a cabin in the woods is the man I am most comfortable with and the man I most want to be.

This book is mostly about that man and the quiet world he fervently seeks.

I offer it here for what I sincerely hope is your reading enjoyment.

— *Steve Hopkins*

The cabin in winter.

Chapter One
AT THE CABIN

Jim Skinnin's Old Place

I never met Jim Skinnin. We missed each other by more than a century.

It's probably just as well because if he were alive today, he'd be pretty mad at me anyway. You see, he worked and sweated to clear a Kickapoo Valley wilderness area and turn it into a farm. I'm letting it grow back to brush.

Jim is the first entry on the Abstract of Title to a piece of land that now belongs to me. It says, simply, "United States to Jim Skinnin, Oct. 22, 1853."

I'll never know what caused him to claim this particular piece of land. As farm land it doesn't amount to much, even now. Possibly there was

5

something about the rugged beauty of it that appealed to him. Maybe it was the challenge of taming 40 acres of wild country and it certainly must have been wild back then.

It would have been solid virgin hardwood forest, a deep valley between two steep ridges, too steep to plow and almost too steep to climb.

It would have been a land inhabited by foxes and deer, squirrels and rabbits and by wolves, black bears and probably even a roaming mountain lion or two.

I climbed the steep west ridge one day not long ago and at the top I sat with my back against an old oak tree. I lit my pipe and I looked down into the valley and across a span of nearly 120 years. I could see Jim down there, hard at work on his cabin in the center of a small clearing. I could see a pile of logs, a wagon box loaded with provisions and simple tools. A team of horses grazed contentedly not far away.

Jim, the sleeves of his homespun cotton shirt rolled above his elbows, was methodically swinging a broadaxe, chips flying as he slowly turned the pile of logs into squared, cabin-size timbers. Occasionally, he would stop and look up at the hills around him. I wondered if his heart was lifted by the sight or if he was cursing the decision that had brought him to this wild and Godforsaken land.

Maybe he was daydreaming of the bride he someday hoped to bring to his homestead. He must have been alone here. Other families would come later to clear the rest of the valley and to build the church and the school that still stand, side by side, on a nearby hill.

But I think Jim must have missed all that because on May 13, 1865, somebody else took over his land for payment of $17.33 in delinquent taxes. I don't know what happened to Jim. Maybe he gave up and drifted on. Maybe he died, leaving no heirs. More than likely, he got caught up in the Civil War and never returned to his Kickapoo homestead.

There still is an old log cabin here and it may have been one Jim built or started. Others followed him on the land and chances are somebody else at least enlarged the cabin and put the tin roof on it. And somebody else cleared the big hilltop meadow and turned it over with a team and a breaking plow. Somebody else's wife must have planted the orchard up by the meadow and proudly watched it bear fruit.

But it's Jim Skinnin I think of mostly when I walk the rugged hillsides up here. I envy him because I wish I could see it as it was 120 years ago, before most of the virgin timber was cut for building and firewood, before civilization drove most of the wild critters away.

That day, I climbed down from the ridge and walked back to my own cabin, one that I built mostly with my own hands.

It was late evening and there was a chill in the air so I started a small fire in the old iron stove. And when the cabin was warm, I poured a glass of homemade wine from a Mason jar and I drank a silent toast to Jim.

I wished I could have known him and talked with him. But, somehow, I was glad he wasn't around to see the day I drove up here in a big black station wagon and sat in a lawyer's office and signed the papers and wrote the check that made the place mine.

Sharing a Dream With Early Settlers

There is something about the Kickapoo Hills that attracted the early settlers, the men and women and their families who came in wagons and on foot from the east by way of Ohio and Kentucky and Tennessee.

If they came in the spring they would have seen lush green hillsides and an abundance of timber to cut for building and for firewood and there were maples that would provide sugar and syrup.

They would have seen springs welling up from the ground and streams, clear and fresh, water to grind their wheat and corn.

There were hilltops and fertile valleys waiting to be cleared. There was land for growing and there was land for grazing. There was wild game in the hills, too, meat for their rough-hewn cabin tables.

A man could not ask for much more then, perhaps even now, than the opportunity to live and work and raise a family in these surroundings.

I feel close to these settlers when I am here now, partly, but not entirely, because my own ancestors were among them.

Do I not share something of their lives? Do not my eyes see the same hills? Is it not the same morning sun that warms my cabin porch? Do not the same mists sometimes settle in the valley in the evening? Does not the thunder rolling through the hills sound the same?

I have walked these hills in all seasons, hills that once felt the tread of moccasin and cobbled boot. My boots are better made, perhaps, and certainly more expensive, but the hills know not the difference, nor do they care. What, after all, is a hundred years to a hill?

I have walked their hillside wagon roads and the meadows where once their crops grew.

I have known the same quiet of the deep woods early in the morning and the same peace that comes with the setting of the evening sun. I have known the same hot summer days and the same long winter nights.

We came here a few years ago, like they did, to build our own cabin.

It was built with hand tools, with hammer and chisel, with brace and bit and with crosscut saw.

A hundred years, I would venture, has not changed the ring of a hammer nor has it altered the rasp of a saw.

We finished the roof one evening just before a thunderstorm broke. The siding was not yet on, but there was a roof over our heads and a floor under our feet.

We moved most of our provisions under the shelter of the roof and that night, with a few friends and neighbors, we had a cabin warming party by lantern light while the thunder echoed through the hills and the rain poured down all around us.

I doubt that any 19th Century family ever was more proud of its handiwork.

I have sat beside a tiny brook here and watched my shadow on the water and wondered whose shadow was there yesterday — and whose will be there tomorrow.

And sometimes when I am working alone, cutting firewood or mending a bit of fence, I can feel the presence of the frontiersmen. I think it is an awareness that I, just as they were, am only a link between past and future and that I have no permanent claim to this land. Their ghostly visits serve to remind me of my temporary role of caretaker. They keep me humble.

My work does not involve the clearing of land, the building of wagon roads and the growing of crops. But just as the land served its purpose for those who came before, it now serves its purpose for me.

I am a writer and though my work is not nearly as strenuous as theirs, it is work nonetheless.

I come here for renewal. I seek the peace and the quiet, the freedom and the space, the reassurance that I find only in the order of the natural world.

Here, I can examine my own beginnings and, in them, I find reassurance, too.

I come here to think and to wonder and to dream.

I am, most of all, a dreamer, and perhaps that is the strongest bond I share with my predecessors.

Was it, after all, anything less than a dream that led them across the wilderness to these hills?

I Feel Hunger, Cold and Pain

It's a cold and blustery weekend and now, at night, it's good to be warm and inside the cabin.

I just returned from a walk up the road. The wind was cold enough on this late March night to cause me to turn my coat collar up and my ear-flaps down. A light, sleet-like snow stung my face and clung to my beard.

It was pitch dark and it seemed that I was alone in a world that consisted solely of a small circle of lantern light.

Back inside now, the radio is telling me that it is snowing and that the night might get down to five below zero. It's only confirming what I already know.

I think the countryman is more sensitive to changes in the natural world than is his city cousin, perhaps because he is more directly affected by such things as sudden changes in the weather. It determines, for instance, whether there will be travel in and out of his lane.

Perhaps the city dweller, aware tonight only of the flickering images on his television set, is unaware of the storm raging without. His drapes are pulled to shield him from the outside. His thermostat will compensate for changes in the temperature.

Here at the cabin I find I am responsible for my own comfort and I know I will be up several times during the night to keep the fire going in the wood stove.

I saw the change in the weather first in the evening sky, I heard it in the howl of the stovepipe and, later, I walked abroad to be part of it.

I sometimes think man is going through an evolutionary process that is alienating him from the natural world; that his instincts for survival, for instance, are becoming more attuned to a mechanical world.

We can walk through the woods in safety. We no longer are threatened by grizzly bears. We are not likely to be attacked and captured by an Indian raiding party. It is not really necessary to be constantly alert for the sound of the snapping of a twig that might spell danger.

The greatest threat to our safety in the modern world is mechanical failure. Imagine driving along a highway and your right rear tire blows out. You feel and hear a sudden change and you instinctively sense what happened. Your reflexes take over. You tighten your grip on the steering wheel, make the necessary compensations and bring your car safely to a stop on the shoulder of the road.

That is the identical instinct, the same reflex that would have warned a frontiersman of a charging bear, that would have caused him to whirl, calmly aim his flintlock, and drop it dead in its tracks.

I suppose it's only natural that man's instincts adjust to the world he has created for himself to live in. But there are those of us who still say: "What's the hurry? Can't we have a little of both worlds? Do we have to destroy the past to build the future?"

Mankind was neither manufactured in Detroit nor was he "Made in Japan." We crawled out of a swamp millions of years ago along with the other creatures that inhabit the earth.

I wonder if there isn't at least a subconscious desire in man to reject this beginning, to deny his fellowship with other creatures. There would be less guilt over his treatment of the buffalo, the passenger pigeon, the grizzly, the timber wolf.

It certainly would ease our minds when we drain a marsh, ravage a mountain, or pollute an ocean.

Perhaps our downfall will lie in convincing ourselves that we are indeed superior beings who can live without the natural world, who can convince ourselves that a balance of nature is unnecessary, that we are supermen who can survive in a radioactive atmosphere without food, water or air.

I am not easily convinced.

I am an animal. I know that I am blood brother to the grizzly, the rattlesnake and the alligator.

I feel hunger, cold and pain. My skin tingles and my heart beats faster when I am startled.

I am usually harmless, but I will fight when I am cornered or when my "cubs" are threatened.

I know that the same instinct that sends a grizzly into hibernation in the fall keeps me inside, close to the warmth of the stove, on a cold winter's night.

Reading this over, I decide it will make a rather strange entry in the Cabin Journal. But, for better or for worse, these are my thoughts on a stormy March night.

Spring Visitors

Sunday, May 5 — The builders are at work. In our absence, the wasps have started nesting under the eaves and once in awhile a stray one will find its way into the cabin.

A barn swallow has built a mud nest again, under the eaves near the back door. Two years ago, in the same place, a swallow nest, loosened maybe by vibration from our opening and closing the door, tumbled to the ground and the freshly-hatched young birds died.

I don't know if the current resident is the same swallow or not, but, if she is, I would think she would have learned her lesson.

Evenings and early mornings still are cool enough for a fire in the wood stove. We let it go out during the night now and it only takes a small fire to take the morning chill out of the air.

I light it as soon as I get up and the cabin is cozy and warm by the time I return from town with the Sunday newspaper.

Down by the truck putting some fishing gear away this morning, I hear Theron Phillip's pickup turn into the lane. Soon I hear his familiar greeting: "I saw your gate chain was down and I thought you might be here." The greeting is kind of a private joke between us.

I put the lawn chairs out by the front steps for the first time this spring and we sit and talk awhile over a cup of coffee. Then we head up the hill for a walk through the woods. My youngest daughter, Jayne, who is 9 now, laces on her new boots and comes along.

The bloodroot is blooming. And there are patches of violets here and there and clusters of Mayapples in the open areas.

There are a few sturdy old trees on the hillside behind the cabin, most of them near the top. The bulk of the growth is small young trees and saplings. A neighbor once told me that 20 years ago there wasn't a tree on the hillside. It had all been cut off for firewood and lumber, he said.

Sometimes, poking around in the woods, I see signs that remind me that others inhabited and owned and worked this land long before it was mine; like the time I found a broken piece of runner from an old stoneboat, half-buried in the humus along the edge of a hillside tote road.

Today, Theron and I are looking for a couple of trees to cut for firewood for the cabin stove. He is better at identifying trees than I am and along the way he points out a couple of young hickories that I didn't know were there. I don't know why, but I am pleased to find that I have hickories on my land.

For cutting, we finally pick two white ash trees and an old white oak all near the edge of the hilltop meadow. We will cut them in another week or two and my son, Pete, and I will spend some spring weekends sawing them into stove lengths and splitting and piling them.

In the fall, after they have seasoned for the summer, Theron will help us haul them down with his four-wheel-drive.

Frances visited Mrs. Mattie Kempf this afternoon, a friendly, smiling Amish lady who lives on a farm near our place. She returned with a quart of maple syrup, fresh from this spring's run, which graced our supper table this evening and added a dash of woodland flavor to our pancakes.

Tonight the noise and confusion of the city seem far away. It is extremely pleasant to be here in the country on this early spring weekend.

(Monday, May 13) — I am here alone this morning. I got up about 5:30 and drove up from Madison to spend a few hours here, but still have to drive back and go to the office this afternoon.

The swallow's nest is still intact and I suspect there are eggs inside. I hope they make it this year.

It starts to storm while I am here, but I am content to putter around inside while the storm rages without.

I light a fire in the stove and settle back to listen to the crackling of the stove pipe and the pounding of the rain on the roof.

One bolt of lightening strikes perilously close and for a fraction of a second the inside of the cabin is an eerie blue. I am surprised when it's over that the lights still are on. I open the cabin door and step out to see if it struck something nearby. There is no sign of damage, but there is a faint smell of ozone in the air.

It must have been on the tail end of the storm which seems to be passing over now.

I go back inside and finish sharpening an axe; then I touch up the edge of my pocketknife, not terribly important, but rather pleasant things to be doing on a rainy morning.

The rain is letting up. Maybe I'll take a walk through the lush, wet spring woods before I drive back to the city.

A Rainy Day Breaks Summer's Heat

Today there is some respite from the heat of mid-summer and I am spending a lazy afternoon on the cabin porch.

It's pouring down rain and I can see it and hear it and smell it, but I am dry and comfortable here, cooled by a breeze that is sweeping up the valley.

I like the view from here at this time of the year. The brush and weeds that surround the cabin have reached their full mid-summer growth. There are berries, for the picking, just outside the back door. A chipmunk is scurrying around in the path by the front steps.

I think of last night and the trip up here from the city and enjoying all the familiar sights and sounds and feelings, the pleasure of leaving the city and driving into the sunset, through the flat Wisconsin River valley towns of Arena and Spring Green and, then, finally, heading into the Kickapoo Hills just outside of Richland Center. The sun had almost disappeared; there was only a red glow from somewhere over the hilltops. Horses and cattle grazed contentedly by the fencelines along the roadside.

It was night when we drove into the cabin lane and I unlocked the gate chain by the light of a full moon. It was good to be back.

It was 60 degrees on the porch thermometer and there was a promise of rain in the night air. I built a small fire in the woodstove.

A field mouse had shredded an old rag on the porch and had made a nest in the remnants of last winter's kindling pile. There were four tiny new-born mice in it.

This morning we moved the nest to the porch door and left it cracked hoping the mouse, who was watching us warily from behind a shovel, would move her brood outside.

When we looked later she had moved them to another corner of the porch. Frances picked up the nest and carefully placed it under an outside woodpile. The mouse ran out the open porch door. Their chances of survival are slim, I suppose, but there was nothing else to do. We don't want a cabin full of mice.

It's raining harder now. Even the rain seems different in the country. I often think I could stay here always. There is little in the city I couldn't turn my back on and walk away from — except, perhaps, my weekly paycheck.

Maybe I would tire of a steady diet of the simple life, but how I enjoy waking up, like this morning, and knowing that the most important thing I have to do all day is find a new grip for my scythe handle.

That gives me an excuse to go to town, which is entirely different than going to the city. I stop at Major's Feed Store. Fred Major doesn't have the grip I want. "We will make one," he says. He picks up an old shovel handle and we head for the workshop in the back of the store.

I take the home-made handle back to the cabin, bolt it on, file the rough edges and the scythe is as good as new.

How's that when you compare it with the look you get from the clerk in the shopping center hardware department, the look that implies: "What do you want a scythe handle for anyway, stupid?"

If he bothers with you at all he might try to sell you a gallon of weedspray instead, one guaranteed to kill all your weeds, your trees, most of the wildlife that happens by and maybe even your wife and children. "That's the modern way, friend. Why break your back swinging a scythe?"

Most city hardware stores are only fancy gift shops masquerading as hardware stores, at least by my definition. I like a smalltown hardware store where you can buy a splitting axe, a length of stovepipe, a five-gallon metal gasoline can, an enameled wash basin, a porcelain chamber utensil, leather work gloves, a jackknife, a piece of rope or a box of shotgun shells.

And there is one final test. If you can't buy a chimney plug — the kind with a picture on it that you stick in the hole in the chimney when you take the stovepipe out for the summer — then it just ain't a hardware store.

So, anyway, thanks to Fred Major, my scythe is fixed.

But it's too wet to use it today. I think I'll just sit here on the porch and listen to the rain and watch the baby mice in the woodpile.

It's been a long time, maybe too long, since I just sat and watched it rain.

A Familar Walk

I have walked in a number of places through the years, but the walks I seem to enjoy most are those in familiar country close to home.

A woods, if it is traveled often and explored thoroughly, kind of grows on you; it becomes as comfortable as an old pair of boots or a baggy corduroy coat.

The one I knew best was an 80-acre hilltop woods that joined my own 40 acres in Vernon County.

It never belonged to me, but I guess I felt like it did. Most of my walks around the cabin began or ended there.

It was at the end of an old wagon road that climbed a hill near the cabin and was separated from my own woods by only a few strands of rusty barbed wire fence.

The man who owned it cut his firewood out of there and the result, through the years, was a network of wide trails that made walking a pleasure.

I never have been one for strenuous hiking, preferring always the quiet stroll, unencumbered by backpacking equipment and I never have felt the necessity to thrash aimlessly around in the brush. If there is a trail, I will follow it gladly and gratefully.

At first, I would enter the woods by bellying under the fence at the end of the wagon road, a practice that ended abruptly one summer day when I found myself eye-to-eye with a coiled hognose snake.

There was an anxious moment until we had determined that each other was harmless. We backed off and went our separate ways. Still, the possibility of another such chance encounter stayed with me and I thereafter found a place where I could cross the fence in an upright position.

The woods was home for deer and for small animals. My son, when he was 12, shot his first squirrel there and later his first ruffed grouse, flushed from the dense thicket along the fenceline.

A profusion of wildflowers grew there in the spring and in the fall. Exquisite coral cup fungus could be found, on occasion, under the dead leaves along the edge of the trails.

The trees were sugar maple and oak and there was some basswood and ironwood and elm and hickory and ash.

One of my favorite perches was a maple stump at the edge of a small clearing near the center of the woods. If I got there early enough on an autumn morning and if I sat there long enough and quietly enough, I would be almost certain to hear the snort of a deer or to catch a glimpse of a pileated woodpecker or a sleek red fox.

The woods was alive with color in the autumn, a bright torch lit by the first rays of the morning sun.

In the winter, the paths became ski trails and I remember gliding through a stark, white land; through a muffled silence disturbed only by the bold cries of the crows.

One day, the owner, who was getting along in years, sold his land, including the woods, and moved to town.

The new owner was a corn farmer from Iowa who saw nothing of value in trees or wildflowers or in woodpeckers or grouse or rabbits or deer.

With saw and bulldozer, he leveled the woods. I wasn't there when it happened, but some of it, I imagine, was sold for lumber; the rest burned or shoved into ditches and buried.

It happened quickly and without my knowledge and I could not have prevented it had I known.

I stumbled on the result one day by accident. I stood by the fence at the end of the wagon road and stared in disbelief at a vast wasteland. It had been raining and what once was a beautiful woods now was an 80-acre sea of mud.

I said goodbye to the woods there and turned my back on it and walked away.

That was over a year ago. I have not returned to check on the corn crop; I hope it was a failure.

Usually, when I walk now, I head in other directions; when I do near the area where the woods used to be, I stay just far enough away so that I cannot see the desolation on the other side of the fence.

But familiar places, like old friends, are not easily forgotten and there are times when I sit on the cabin porch and imagine the woods is still there, beckoning.

I climb the hill once more then and cross the fence — and I walk it again in my mind.

Autumn Fire

There is a feeling in October that the soft, golden Indian summer days will linger forever, that there is no need to hurry. Then, suddenly, the golden autumn is swept away by a harsh north wind and we are reminded that winter is almost upon us.

Most of the work at the cabin here is finished. The crop from the garden is harvested. The walnuts and the hickory and butternuts have been picked and stored.

But we look at the cabin wood supply now and know that stove wood has to be split and stacked neatly on the porch and soon, or we'll be digging it out of the snow.

The first thing I do when we get up here now is start the big wood-burning stove. It's a chore that gives me great pleasure, possibly because it gives me a chance to recreate the kitchen range and wood stove days of my boyhood.

It starts with shaking down the ashes and dumping them outside. Then the fire is built carefully. The crumpled wads of newspaper are laid in the firebox first, then a few pieces of aspen kindling from a pile behind the stove.

Now, with the chimney damper and the draft at the bottom of the stove both wide open, the fire is lit. When the kindling gets a good start, I add a few pieces of maple or butternut and then, finally, a couple of big chunks of white oak.

The stove howls as the draft whips up the flames. The wood snaps and pops, and the expanding metal in the chimney begins to crackle. The cabin warms up slowly as the heat is absorbed by the walls and floor and furniture. The windows begin to steam up and the cabin is comfortable and cozy now.

The chimney damper and bottom draft are shut down and the draft on the firebox door is opened. Now the fire will be fed by oxygen drawn across the top of it instead of up through it and it will burn more slowly. The water can, a five gallon milk can which is a chunk of ice now, is set close to the stove to thaw.

With the cabin chores done, Pete, my 12-year-old Daniel Boone, and I pick up our shotguns and head for the woods. We often spend a good part of the day there, sometimes hunting, mostly walking.

The jays begin to scold as soon as we enter the woods, warning all the wildlife of our presence. At the top of the first hill a ruffed grouse flushes behind us. Startled by the roar of its ascent, we turn in time to watch it disappear into the brush. We walk on, through the old apple orchard. There are about a half-dozen aged trees left there, all bent and dying. I never pass it without thinking of the pleasure it once must have brought to the family of pioneers who lived in the old log cabin in the valley below.

Beyond the orchard two more grouse flush from a patch of sumac that is reaching out into the meadow. We shoot at these and miss. We miss a few more before we return to the warmth of the cabin.

Night comes early in the woods now and we spend more time in the cabin than during the spring and summer months. After supper, with the cabin chores done, the chairs are drawn close to the comfort of the fire.

Tomorrow there is work to be done, a stone wall to be laid up to keep the hillside from reclaiming a corner of the cabin.

But tonight we sit by the stove and read while the children play on the hooked rug nearby and the dog dozes and dreams in her favorite spot between the stove and the wall, a scene that has been familiar in cabins and farm homes for more than two centuries.

Winter's Chill

How good it feels to wake up in the morning and look out the cabin window and see snow falling on the hills outside.

Yesterday it rained all day and into the night, a cold depressing late

November rain that blew into the porch through the screen, soaked the woodpile stacked there and dampened everything else around, including the spirit.

Now the outside and the porch and the woodpile have frozen dry, the eaves have ceased their incessant dripping, the world this morning is crisp and fresh and brand new. The spirit, being as malleable as potting clay, has revived.

It is the last day of November. The thermometer outside says it is 14 degrees above zero.

I let the fire go out during the night and the inside of the cabin is as cold as the outside. I am faced with the task of getting it started again.

Shivering in my longjohns and hopping from one cold foot to the other, I stuff the stove with paper and kindling and dump in a half a bean can of diesel oil. I toss in a lighted kitchen match and slam the door before the mess blows up in my face. I am not one of these purists who monkeys around with flint and steel.

The flames roar up the chimney and the cabin slowly begins to warm. I dress close to the stove and hold my boots upside down above it to warm them before putting them on.

The rest of the family soon is up and dressed. Having spent a rainy Saturday inside, we all are suffering a little from cabin fever. We take an informal vote and decide on a walk in the woods before breakfast.

It is the last day of the deer hunting season, and we search for all the red, orange and yellow garments we can find.

It is, it seems to me, a sad commentary on the deer hunter when even those who determine the rules of the hunt agree that the hunter can't tell a man from a deer unless the man is dressed in bright gaudy colors and sometimes not even then.

I always am glad when the deer season is over and the walker once again can be safe in the woods without dressing like a clown.

We are a strange appearing crew when we head up the hill behind the cabin. There is a red bandanna pinned to a hat. There are a couple of red shirts stretched tightly over down jackets.

The snow still is falling and there is a chill, biting wind.

About a year ago I cut some firewood near the top of the hill, and there is a heavy butt end of a white ash still lying there near a brush pile. I have been wanting to get it down to the cabin where I can use it for a chopping block.

This morning Pete and I stand it on edge and push it off on a long, narrow, fairly clear trajectory down the hillside. It rolls and bumps and wobbles along until it finally hits a tree and comes to a stop about halfway down.

Later, when our route takes us back that way again, we will roll it the rest of the way down the hill and lug it to the cabin woodpile.

Now we walk on.

Our walk has a goal. We are looking for a sturdy thorn apple sapling for my father to dry and peel and shape into a stout walking staff.

There are differences of opinion, among walkers, about walking staffs.

Colin Fletcher, the well-known hiker, backpacker and author of "The Complete Walker," says he will not be without one.

"For many years now, it has been a third leg to me — and much more besides," he writes.

British walker John Hillaby, who not long ago made a 1,300-mile solitary trek across Europe, disdains the use of a staff. "A good walker is a biped, not a tripod," he maintains.

I like a walking stick and find it invaluable, especially for balance in hilly country. It provides balance and braking ability on steep descents, and it provides leverage on a climb, transferring some of the load from the legs to the shoulders and arms. A walking staff also is a good defense against vicious dogs.

My walking staff, which I have carried for years, was cut from a sumac sapling. Sumac is not the strongest wood, but it is strong enough for my needs, it is light and it has served me well.

We find the thorn apple we are looking for and I cut it with a small saw I am carrying.

There are morning chores to be done back at the cabin. The beds have to be made, the floor needs a good sweeping, the woodpile on the porch needs replenishing.

Frances and Kate and Jayne tackle the inside chores. Pete and I are at work on the new chopping block by the outside woodpile when the cabin door opens and the odor of bacon and eggs drifts out.

"Breakfast is ready," Frances says.

There is nothing like a cold, snowy morning for reviving the spirit.

Country Lessons

A man who spends some of his time living in a cabin in the woods soon becomes aware that his cabin habits differ greatly from his city habits.

19

There are, if he pays attention, a number of lessons he can learn from this, largely lessons in economy. He will find that he develops a different attitude toward waste, because waste in a cabin in the woods will cause him extra problems and extra work.

A man who carries his water from a spring nearly a half-mile away is not likely to use it indiscriminately. A man who cuts and hauls his own firewood learns to use it wisely. A man who has to dispose of his own trash by hauling it three miles to a town dump becomes careful about filling his trash can. A man living with a wife and three children in an 18-by-24 foot cabin learns that life there is much less complicated if their material possessions are limited to necessities.

He discovers that, in these areas, money is of little or no use to him. He can't buy rubbish pickup where it doesn't exist or water or fuel where there are no water mains or natural gas lines to hook into.

So he does the best he can. He discovers that a little water will go a long way, that water can be saved by doing dishes only once a day, that rinse water can be used again for wiping up the floor and other cleaning jobs. He finds he can keep himself reasonably clean using only a small basin of warm water.

A good countryman learns to husband his woodpile and he learns how to get the most from his stove. He soon discovers which woods will burn rapidly and which will burn more slowly and provide a bed of glowing, long-lasting coals. He learns to save the big chunks of white oak for nighttime burning. If he doesn't learn these things he finds that his woodpile is rapidly diminishing, long before the heating season is over.

He learns to put his ashes out where they can be plowed back into the garden in the spring. Some of the garbage gets set out for birds and other wildlife; the rest is buried. Waste paper is used to kindle the stove. Jars and flattened cans are the only waste that ever reaches the dump.

Eventually, he realizes that he has found a great deal of personal satisfaction in his ability to manage his own environment.

If he has learned these cabin lessons well, he will begin to apply them to his home in the city. He might spend some time thinking about where his heat comes from, where his water comes from, and where his rubbish goes.

And, if he does, he will think twice before setting his thermostat on 75 degrees and leaving it there, before he wastes his water simply because it is available in seemingly endless supply. He certainly should wonder why, once a week, he sets several overloaded trash cans at his curb for the rubbish trucks to pick up and haul away.

He will begin to understand that, as a consumer, he is responsible for the resources he consumes. The fact that he isn't quite sure where they came from in the first place or that he isn't quite sure where the rubbish truck will take them doesn't make him any less responsible.

He has learned to accept the responsibility for his environment at the cabin. When he learns to accept it in the city, it will be the beginning of a better way of life.

Peter Hopkins on the Wolf River.

Chapter Two
FATHERS AND SONS

A Man Fishes to Find a Boy

It is nearing evening on a bright, warm Saturday in June when the man in a beat-up old yellow truck turns off the blacktop road and heads down a set of deeply rutted sand tracks toward a familiar stretch of stream.

He has not really planned to fish on this day, but his fishing gear is in the back of the truck, and now, suddenly, he feels the need to be here, in this place.

He will wade the stream and he will fish, but it is not a trout he will be seeking. He knows it is foolish, maybe, but he has come here mostly to try to find a boy.

He came here for the first time with the boy four years ago, when the boy was 12. He remembers that time and how the boy looked in his first pair of chest-waders that were folded over at the knees because they were too large for him. He remembers the three small, sparkling brown trout the boy caught and he remembers the boy holding them up proudly for him to see.

They had fished here and in other places since, but for the last couple of years they had not fished together as often because the boy was growing up and had other things to do.

The truck stops where the road ends in the woods and the man gets out and takes his flyrod from the back. He attaches a reel, strings the heavy flyline through the guides, ties on a leader and knots a small coachman fly on the end of it. He pulls on his waders and starts down the path to where he will enter the stream.

He remembers the morning when he went into the boy's room where the boy was packing to leave for a job at a summer camp. The boy was 16 now. It would be his first summer away from home.

The man's old Air Force duffel bag, stuffed full of clothing and gear, was on the bed. His name and serial number, stenciled on the bag about 25 years before, still stood out sharply against the faded olive drab.

"I haven't seen that for awhile," the man said.

"Lift it," the boy said. "It's heavy."

"I know," the man answered. "I carried it once for a long time, when I was not much older than you are now."

Beside the duffel bag were a small overnight bag, a rolled sleeping bag and a guitar. They carried them out and loaded them in the truck.

The boy kissed his mother and said goodbye to his sisters and got into the truck on the driver's side. The man climbed into the passenger seat beside him.

The man had started to teach the boy to drive a long time before on the graveled town roads in western Wisconsin. The boy, at first, would sit on his lap and steer. Later, when the boy could reach the pedals, the man sat beside him and instructed him patiently.

The boy was a good driver now and the man was relaxed riding with him.

They drove north, out of the rich southern Wisconsin farmland and into the central sand country where the land flattens out and where miles of crystal-clear trout streams wind through forests of scrub oak and poplar and pine.

"This will be good country for you to spend the summer in," the man said.

"Yes," the boy answered, "I like it here. I always liked it when we came here to fish."

"The Mayflies will be hatching soon and the fishing will be good," the man said.

"I know," the boy answered. "I'll miss that this year."

They crossed a stream, near the spot where the man was fishing now. "Remember the night I had a big brown one in there, and you slid down the bank and into the water in the dark and netted it for me?," the boy asked.

"Yes," the man replied. "I remember."

"We've had some good times," the boy said.

"Yes," the man said, "we've had some good times. I've enjoyed every minute while you were growing up and now I am very proud of you."

At the camp, they carried the boy's gear to his room and dumped it on a bunk. When the man drove away, he looked in the rear-view mirror and saw the boy standing there, talking intently with the camp director. The boy did not look up.

The man felt strange driving away alone and leaving him there, but he knew he would have to get used to that. He would never again have the boy all to himself.

The man picks his way through a tangle of alders now and steps into the stream. He feels the firm, sand bottom underfoot and the coolness of it rushing against his legs.

There is a trout in the first bend, and then there is another and another. He is not carrying a net and he puts them all carefully back in the water.

After a while, he climbs out of the stream onto a high bank and watches the deep pool below, the same pool where the boy caught the brown trout that night a few years ago.

For an instant, he thinks he sees the boy in the baggy waders there but he can't hold the image in his mind, and he sees, instead, the young man he just left behind.

He remembers the old duffel bag and the years when he was young and eager to be on his own. He wonders where the years have gone.

He stands to go and turns and looks once more at the stream.

"So long, Son," he says, aloud. "Have a good summer."

He walks slowly back up the path to the truck.

Squirrel-hunting on the Homestead

There is a small hardscrabble farm in a valley in Richland County that I often find myself thinking about with the approach of autumn and the hunting season.

The farm belonged to my grandparents. My father was raised there. I used to spend summers there when I was a boy.

It wasn't much of a farm then and it isn't now. But there was a time when I thought it was the greatest place in the world.

The house was small, but comfortable. It had started out as a one-room log cabin, but the addition of other rooms long ago obscured the original log building.

It wasn't until some time in the 1940s that the kerosene lamps were replaced by electricity. For as long as I can remember, the water came from a kitchen sink pump. The cooking always was done on an old-fashioned wood range.

A gravel road and a huge stone gate separated the house from the barn and, on the other side of the barn, was a spring from which flowed the coldest, sweetest water in the valley.

On both sides of the valley, behind the house and behind the barn, steep wooded hillsides stretched toward the sky.

It was these hills that my father hunted as a lad. And one fall day, a couple of years ago, he said he'd like to go up there and roam those hills and hunt for squirrels just once more.

So, on a crisp, clear October morning, we drove up to the old homestead and knocked on the door. A stranger answered. She stood on the porch, right where my grandmother used to stand when she threw the dishwater at the cats, and she gave us permission to hunt on her property.

"Mind if we look the place over?" we asked.

"Go right ahead," she said, and disappeared back into the house.

The place no longer was being farmed. The new residents were only using the house.

The stone gate, which my grandfather had worked so hard to build, was beginning to crumble. The banks of the spring had caved in and what once was a beautiful clear pool now was only a puddle. The brook that once sprung from it had dwindled to a tiny trickle.

We climbed the hill and crossed to the other side to the valley my father wanted to see again. It was much like he remembered, except that an automobile junkyard down the road had begun spilling into the valley from the far end.

We sat on the hillside in the sunshine, Dad and I, and we talked about things like growing up and change and progress. And a father passed on to his son some of the treasured memories from his past.

Later, we walked across the side of the hill and into the woods where we hunted for the rest of the morning. This, too, had changed. The woods were the same, the squirrels had gone.

It was nearing noon and we were getting ready to give up when we finally cornered one in the crotch of an old oak.

Dad was on one side of the tree; I was up above him on the other side.

I watched Dad raise his .22 to his shoulder and squint through the iron sights. He hesitated, then lowered the gun.

"You shoot him if you want to," he said. "I can't."

I tucked my own rifle back into the crook of my arm. "Let's leave him be," I answered.

So we turned our backs on the lone squirrel in the old oak tree and we walked, side by side, out of the woods.

I think we learned something that day — about ourselves and about each other.

Playing Hooky

I was sitting in the office the other day, looking through a stack of mail that had piled up while I was away on vacation, and I came across a copy of the Ducks Unlimited magazine.

I started thumbing through it. There were pages of color reproductions of paintings by Maynard Reece and other wildlife artists; there were waterfowling articles and shotgun and decoy advertisements.

Soon, I was daydreaming of crisp autumn mornings. I could hear the splash of decoys being tossed out of a skiff in the pre-dawn half-light. In my mind's eye, I could see their silhouettes bobbing gently in the water just off a grassy point. I imagined waiting, hidden in the wet reeds, for dawn and the first flock of ducks to come gliding in.

It suddenly came to me that this was the middle of August, that summer was quietly slipping away.

I turned a page and there was a photograph of Artist Reece, sketch pad in hand, sitting in a canoe that was anchored in a patch of lily pads.

That did it. I put all the mail back in a stack and stuck it in a drawer — and I went fishing.

THE QUIET WORLD OF STEVE HOPKINS

I stopped by the house to pick up Pete, and, in less than an hour, we were down on Mt. Vernon Creek.

Pete is 14 now and his summer is slipping away, too. When he goes back to school this fall, it will be to a high school. This boy who has been my partner for all these years is becoming a young man.

I didn't tell him, but I was more interested in watching him that day than I was in fishing myself. I sat on the tailgate of the truck and loaded my camera while he climbed into his waders. I watched him fasten a leader to the end of his flyline and expertly knot on a fly.

"Which way do you want to go, Pete?" I asked.

"I think I'll start at the bridge and work up towards town," he answered.

"Okay," I said. "I'll go downstream aways and start there."

I stood on a small footbridge and watched him go, wading up the stream until it got too deep and he had to take to the bank.

I watched him carefully placing his backcast to avoid snagging his fly in the brush. My thoughts went back to the days when I seemed to spend most of my fishing time helping him untangle his lines. It didn't seem long ago at all.

I remembered other fishing trips, mornings and evenings on a stream. I remembered a rainy opening day a few years ago when he headed off downstream by himself and was gone so long that I began to worry about him. I went looking for him and when I found him he was sitting happily on the bank, soaking wet, with three or four nice brown trout lying in the grass beside him.

I remembered the look on his face when he caught his first lunker bass up in the St. Croix Flowage and the excitement until we finally got it into the canoe.

Now, I stood on the bridge until he disappeared around the first bend; then I got my own flyrod and headed for the stream. I worked my way through the shoulder-high grass and the clouds of mosquitos to a deep pool at a bend in the stream. I tied on a nymph and flicked it out and into the water. Then I began to retrieve it slowly, inch by inch.

I lit my pipe, and I thought about summers and about boys growing up to be men.

There was a splash at the end of my leader, but I reacted too late and the trout was gone.

I really didn't care.

Summer Fishing and a Thunderstorm

It was dusk and I was drifting a dry fly across a small pool on a cow pasture stream up in Vernon County. I could see upstream to where Pete was approaching another pool on his hands and knees. I watched him hesitate a few moments at the edge, then carefully drop a White Wulff over the bank and onto the water about five feet below.

A small brown trout flashed out from the undercut bank and struck it. Pete played it out expertly, deftly moving the rod tip to keep the brown from returning to the tangle of roots under the bank. Then, when there was no more fight left in the brown, he raised it up over the bank, removed the hook from its lip, and slid his prize into the pocket of his fishing vest.

Without a word, he moved on upstream and disappeared into the night, somewhere on the other side of a herd of grazing Holsteins. I watched him go, proudly but with a twinge of sadness, because I realized, for maybe the first time, that he was growing up.

A few days later we were fishing on the Mecan River in Waushara County. Pete was upstream and I was down and we were separated by maybe a quarter of a mile of water when a sudden thunderstrom blew in from the west. It was nearly dark and the deep holes in the Mecan make the footing treacherous for even a grown man in waders. Pete was only a boy in hip boots and I started wading up the winding, brush-lined stream to find him.

There was no sign of him, and I couldn't find the spot where I'd entered the stream. So I got out anyway and started through the brush to where I thought the truck was parked. I thrashed around in the woods for five minutes or more and found myself back on the river, downstream from where I'd gotten out.

I started upstream again and had gone only a few feet when I heard a voice from around the next bend holler: "Dad, up this way!" He'd been worried about me. And he'd found me.

I guess I saw the beginnings of his approaching manhood last summer when his horse broke out of a pack string in the Swan Mountain Range in Montana and headed back toward the ranch at a full gallop. Before I could get to Pete, he'd gotten his horse stopped and turned around by himself and was headed back up the mountain.

We've been bumming around together for quite a few years now, Pete and I, but it doesn't seem long ago that I used to lead him by the hand

and put the worms on his hook for him. Now he ties my trout flies for me.

It's hard to let go. A father, selfishly, would like to keep the idyllic father and son relationship going on forever, but the natural order of things doesn't allow that. So the man will grow older and the boy will grow older and, eventually, the boy will have sons of his own. I wouldn't have it any other way.

I know we'll be good friends when he's a grown man. But I know, too, that there will be times, years from now, when I'll look at him and still see the grinning, freckle-faced boy that found me that night during the thunderstorm on the Mecan.

Only Yesterday

Forgive me if I am a little sentimental, but I am facing something I have not had to deal with before.

It isn't something I would change if I could, because it is as natural as the ebbing and flowing of the tides and it happens just as surely as winter gives away to spring.

It has something to do with a boy becoming a man, and with another man growing a little older. It has something to do with a strange mixture of joy and pain.

The time has come, you see, for my son, the oldest child, to leave home and begin to make his own way in the world.

I guess I always knew it would happen someday, but, dammit all, did it have to happen so soon?

Wasn't it only yesterday that we took the training wheels off his bicycle?

There are so many things we haven't done. Did I prepare him properly for this? Did I teach him everything he has to know? Did we really talk enough during all those years, or wasn't it necessary? Was it enough just to be together?

I remember something he said, shortly after he graduated from high school last spring and announced that he wanted to go out west and look for a job rather than go on to college in the fall.

"I don't want to get out of high school," he said, "and go right to college and start a job and then find out someday that's all there ever was. Maybe I'll go back to school in a couple of years, but not now."

I couldn't argue with that; it's the same way I felt when I was his age, when I bummed around at odd jobs and ended up in the Air Force in Alaska and finally found myself a college freshman at the age of 24. The years between high school and college were good years.

"If that's what you want to do, I guess that's best," I told him. "I think it's what we used to call sowing your wild oats."

"I suppose that's what it is," he said.

"Where do you plan to go, Peter?" I asked.

"Out West, I guess. Probably Montana first, maybe California. I'd like to work in a ski area next winter and spend a summer working in a national park and, if it works out, I might try to get a job on a ranch for awhile. I know I don't want to work inside, in an office."

I suppose I am proud that he can get along without me now, but it hurts just a little.

Wasn't it only yesterday that I showed him how to put a worm on a fishhook? Wasn't it only yesterday that I knelt in the snow to tighten the straps on his snowshoes?

It's hard to let go.

I remember the early years, when he was anxious to be on his own, and I would try to stay in the background and not interfere. But I was never far away if he needed me.

I remember when he was too small to wade the Wolf River, but somehow managed to make it out to a boulder in the middle of the river and stood on top of it in his first pair of hipboots, working his flyrod, with the wild water swirling all around him. He didn't know it then, but I had carefully positioned myself downstream from him, just in case.

The time came when I couldn't follow him everywhere he went, when he had his own friends, and Dad didn't always fit into the picture.

But wasn't it only yesterday that I handed him the keys and said, "Here, son, take the car?" And wasn't it only yesterday that we proudly watched the first smile after the braces came off his teeth?

Sometimes it's easier to say, "No," than it is to say, "Go ahead and try it." But overprotection encourages fear and timidity.

So I said, "Yes," the first time he took a rifle and went into the woods alone. I said, "Yes," a few years ago when he asked permission to go with some friends on a white water canoe trip. And I said, "Yes," when, after his junior year in high school, he announced that he wanted to ride his bicycle up to Bayfield County and back.

I said, "Yes," when he wanted to ski in Montana during the Christmas vacation last year. I said, "Yes," when he and a couple of friends wanted to drive to Florida during the Easter holidays.

He returned safely from all these expeditions, and I knew that my faith in him was justified.

31

Now he is 18 and ready to leave the nest.

I envy him because I remember what it was like to be 18, with your whole life still ahead of you.

I have thought of a lot of last-minute advice to offer, but I won't give it because he doesn't really want or need it.

"It can be a hard world, Peter," I said the other day, "but then I guess it always was. Does it worry you?"

"No," he answered, "not really."

I know that I can't live his life for him, nor can I relive my own life through him. So I guess the time has come to let go of the final string.

Sometime this week he will pack his bag and get on a bus and head for Montana.

I will wish him well and tell him to write and remind him to call his mother once in awhile. And I will tell him his mother and I will always be here should he ever need us.

Wasn't it only yesterday that I told him I loved him?

Peter Hopkins at a winter camp.

Chapter Three

CANOES, SNOWSHOES AND A CLIMB

Paddling and Portaging Boundary Waters

Ely, Minn. — There are five of us on the mile-long portage trail to Little Gabbro Lake, a small and shallow lake in the Boundary Waters Canoe Area.

It has been raining for several days and the trail is a blend of mud, tangled roots and rock. It is quiet. The only sounds are footsteps and an occasional "thunk" when a piece of gear bumps against a tree or a rock. The rain, for the moment at least, has stopped — but it is early morning and there is a mist that hangs heavily in the air.

Paul Eilrick and Ernie Seliskar, both Boundary Waters fishing guides, are carrying 17-foot aluminum canoes on their shoulders.

Don Swenson, retired, from White Bear Lake, Minn., spends summers, with his wife, in a trailer near Ely. He began making a walleye lure, which he has named the "Swen Donka," as a hobby and it has turned into a popular seller in some area resorts and bait shops.

Don, just ahead of me on the trail, is carrying a packboard from which is hung an assortment of gear ranging from boat cushions to cooking pots and pans. Walking easily for a man of 62, he looks for all the world like a lost itinerant peddler.

Louis "Fritz" Warrick, a Madison physician, is our expedition film-maker. He is loaded with camera gear. He also is carrying a large, long-handled fishing net and all of our fishing poles, which have been taped together into a solid bundle.

I carry a large, gray canvas canoe pack loaded with other expedition essentials that seems to weigh 100 pounds, but, in fact, may weigh only 80 or so. In addition, I carry six canoe paddles and part of the equipment necessary for lashing two canoes together.

The trail winds through deep forest that opens into a wide, grassy area where it approaches the lake. Paul and Ernie already are starting to lash the canoes together when I arrive.

Canoes loaded, we begin paddling across Little Gabbro to the big lake. We cross a patch of wild rice and pick our way through a maze of glacial boulders.

This is the Canadian Shield, the exposed skeleton of the earth.

Two young men are camped on a rocky point where Little Gabbro enters Big Gabbro. They are busy trying to dry their gear over a smoky, wet wood fire and they wave glumly when we paddle past.

The wind strikes us when we hit the big lake. There are whitecaps and the waves are growing. We bend our backs and begin paddling into the wind, heading for a small island at the far end of the lake. Our world now is a world of silence, of sky and water and muted green shoreline.

The late Sigurd Olson, writer, environmentalist and one of the most vital forces in the battle to preserve the Boundary Waters as a wilderness, has written that silence includes all natural sounds — "the rushing of water, the crashing of waves against the shore, the roar of avalanches on mountain slopes, the wind through the trees, the howling of wolves . . .

"I believe mechanical equipment of all kinds should be kept out of the wilderness, for it is foreign to silence," he wrote.

The BWCA, sometimes called the Quetico-Superior, includes more than one million acres of wilderness canoe country. It was won after a long and difficult environmental battle and it stretches for 150 miles along the Minnesota-Canadian border and includes more than 1,000 lakes that are

10 acres or larger. It is part of the Superior National Forest. There is a similar wilderness area in Quetico Provincial Park on the Canadian side.

The BWCA is a concept that pleases canoemen and environmentalists. It is not a concept that pleases everyone.

Guide Paul Eilrich wears an Australian bush hat with a big green and blue button pinned to it that proclaims: "Keep the BWCA Open to Everyone."

Paul's reasoning transcends philosophical concepts; it is based on simple fact — he spends most of his working life on the water and, at 51, he would rather run a motorboat than paddle a canoe. He also believes he loses business because some of his fishermen are afraid of canoe travel.

Paul is not a stranger to the wilderness and he is not a once- or twice-a-year visitor. He lives, with his wife, Gladys, on the fringe of the wilderness, deep in the woods in a cabin he built himself from roughsawn lumber cut on the land.

Not long ago his wife shot a black bear out of a tree just outside the cabin. Two of his best hunting dogs have been killed by wolves. It's not an easy life as it is and he does not look too kindly upon those who are trying to make it more difficult.

The sounds of the motorboat and the snowmobile and the roar of the chainsaw are music to his ears. They make his life just a little easier.

It is about 10 a.m. when we make the island, and we paddle into a bay that is somewhat sheltered from the bite of the wind. It is a cold, gray and sunless day.

Paul wanted to fish in a different bay, but he explains that the wind would make that impossible.

"The fish might be a littler smaller in here," he says, "but there will be fish."

The first fish in the boat was a northern caught by Ernie, better-known to his friends as "Oilcan Harry." Ernie is an Ely native, an electrician by trade and a willing volunteer when Paul needs guiding help.

By late afternoon, when we head for home, we have an assortment of northerns, walleyes and crappies, some of which we kept and some of which made a delicious shore lunch at noon.

The wind has picked up during the day and the spray is dashing against the rocks on the shoreline. There are 2-foot waves on the big lake and the wind is at our backs.

The two canoes, lashed together, make a stable and sturdy craft and riding the crests of the waves is a thrill not unlike riding a wild and watery roller coaster.

Once, when I turn to look back, the small island has all but disappeared. Paul tells us later we made the crossing of both lakes in record time — 34 minutes.

On the return portage we are accompanied by the rumble of thunder and long, jagged flashes of lightning.

We stow the gear in Paul's old truck, climb inside and slam the doors just as the storm hits.

We watch it in quiet comfort. It is good, once again, to be warm and dry.

A Trip with Huckleberry Aboard

It is always a pleasure to wake up to find that the weather forecast from the previous night was wrong and that the day that is dawning is sunny and bright and filled with the promise of warmth.

It was so one morning last week and I watched the sun appear while I was puttering around in the back yard, checking the bird feeder and putting fresh water in the birdbath.

Back in the house I filled a stainless-steel vacuum bottle with fresh, black coffee and began rounding up gear I might need for a morning on the water — canoe paddle, life vest, extra sweater, wool gloves (for early morning paddling) and binoculars.

I stopped to pick up Ron Seely a little before 6 a.m. Our destination was a stretch of Wisconsin River backwater along Highway 60 between Sauk City and Spring Green.

There was no good reason for our being on the river on this morning. There didn't have to be. It was enough that it was quiet and out of the way and that it smelled like spring.

Huck Finn said it first — maybe. "It was kind of solemn," he said, "drifting down the big, still river, laying on our backs looking up at the stars, and we didn't even feel like talking loud, and it warn't often that we laughed — only a little kind of a low chuckle. We had mighty good weather as a general thing, and nothing ever happened to us at all."

This is a good time, in the early spring while the river is high and flooding, for being in the bottomlands, in the backwaters and the sloughs. There are more areas accessible now by canoe, more country to travel.

Ron has this old plastic canoe that looks like it once might have been a consolation prize at a used Tupperware drawing. But it is wide of beam and buoyant and it is a good canoe for relaxing in.

We paddled it up the mouth of a feeder creek and then into a still stretch of backwater where we let the canoe drift into a pile of old stumps and anchor itself there. We settled back to watch, to soak up the morning. Somebody has to do it.

Ahead of us a muskrat worked its way slowly from one muddy bank to another. High above, several turkey vultures circled lazily over Ferry Bluff riding the thermals, wings barely moving, at times almost motionless.

Turkey vultures are the only Wisconsin raptors that feed entirely on carrion. They appeared to be watching us and seemed to lose interest when one of us moved.

There were red-winged blackbirds, noisily protesting our intrusion into their nesting territories. There were ducks, mostly mallards, that would fly low above us, wings beating rapidly, in groups of two or three.

Around us was the flood plain, the bottom-land forest, the water-marked silver maple and the river birch, the swamp white oak, the cottonwood and the willow.

Somehow in the spring, the natural world is at its most natural. This is where the rites of spring are performed. This is where the ruffed grouse drums and where the woodcock exhibits its wild, spiraling sky dance.

Ron had brought a casting rod with him that lay, unjointed, in the bottom of the canoe. He never picked it up. Even the shriek of a reel would have broken the spell.

This was not the time, anyway, for disturbing the delicate balance of the river bottom. Man, I believe, has done enough damage; it is time to begin undoing some of it. It is time, perhaps, to let the wild things live in peace — maybe even help them a little.

About mid-morning we picked up our paddles and began working our way downstream. And when we had put the canoe on top of the car and secured it there, we sat awhile on the riverbank and finished the coffee that was still lukewarm in the thermos.

It had been a good morning, and, like our old friend Huckleberry, nothing had really happened to us at all.

An Easy Climb From Behind the Desk

It's a long, steep hike up the CCC Trail from the parking lot to the climbing area along the east bluff at Devils Lake State Park.

The trail winds up a talus slope and it's not a climb in the classic sense, but the "Climber's Guide to Devils Lake" rates it an F1, the easiest climb on a scale of F1 to F10C. The more difficult climbing comes later.

I'm carrying 150 feet of bright orange nylon rope, coiled and slung over my back.

Frances, my wife, is carrying a pack with lunch and the rest of the climbing gear — carabiners, chocks, nylon webbing, climbing harnesses, helmet, leather gloves for rappelling.

We move slowly up the trail, admiring the view as we climb higher and higher above the valley floor, climbing out of the tree tops until, finally, we are standing far above them. We are surrounded by rock now, Baraboo quartzite that began forming during the pre-Cambrian era 1.5 billion years ago, maybe more.

This is a Sunday, a cool, breezy, sunny day, the first after several days of storms and tornadoes that have been sweeping the state.

The young climbers are out in full force at the top of the CCC Trail, spread out with their colorful gear along some of the more difficult climbs, the sheer rock faces — Brinton's Buttress, Pedestal Buttress, Guillotine. We pass them, halting now and then to watch them feel for invisible finger and toe holds as they work slowly and surely up the vertical walls.

We're headed for the Red Rocks area, along the Potholes Trail, where there are some good beginner climbs, most of which we have made before.

We cross the top of the bluff and start down the Potholes Trail, so named because of a series of smooth potholes worn into the quartzite by a pre-historic waterfall. The trail is wet now, almost a waterfall again, carrying the runoff of recent rains.

There are several climbs in the 30- to 40-foot range in the Red Rocks area. We walk up through the trees along the edge of the rock face and unload our gear at the top. The wide, green valley is spread out below us. We can see the south end of Devils Lake in the distance.

Except to go home to sleep Friday night, I have been in the office working on tornado coverage from 4 a.m. Friday to 10 p.m. Saturday. I need this now, the sun, the quiet, the space, the hard use of muscles that have been too long cramped in a desk chair.

I sprawl out on the pine duff and stare at the sky while Frances rummages around in her pack. Soon she offers me a Swiss cheese sandwich, a bag of grapes, some cherries, a dill pickle. We eat, washing it down with gulps from our water bottles.

With lunch over, we begin rigging up a belay. We run nylon webbing from two trees and a rock to insure triple protection for the climber. I snap them all together along with the climbing rope into a set of carabiners and drop the rope over the rock face to the ground.

The rope will be there now to belay the climber on the way up and for rappelling back down again.

We walk to the bottom, snap Frances onto the rope and she begins working her way up the wall, jamming toes, fists and elbows into cracks in the rock where no other holds are available. She is soon at the top.

I make it about half-way up the same wall before I give up and rope down again. I make another nearby climb, up a corner where I work from one wall to another and back again. It is my one successful climb for the day. Frances makes two more before we quit.

In the late afternoon we coil the rope and pack up our gear. Most of the other climbers have gone. The few that are left have finished climbing and are sitting on the rocks in small groups, talking quietly. It is a nice, peaceful place to be, up here.

Back at the bottom I sit on top of a picnic table near the old CCC barracks and sip from a cold bottle of beer while I change from heavy climbing boots to comfortable sneakers.

Frances joins me and, together, we sit in the quiet and watch evening fill the valley.

The Geophysicist and the Scribe

It seems there are no good places to put canoes into rivers and that we are always dragging them down steep muddy banks, around cement bridge pilings and through thick patches of poison ivy.

It is a condition, I suppose, that helps keep rivers in a semi-wild state and almost guarantees a quiet and peaceful experience on even a southern Wisconsin river trip.

On Memorial Day, we slide the canoe down a muddy bank along the Baraboo River, just upstream from where it empties into the Wisconsin.

The Baraboo here is fairly wide and relatively free of sharp bends. The paddling is easy, scarcely more than a drift with an occasional dip of the paddle to keep the bow headed downstream.

There is, for the most part, flat river bottom on either side. The banks are muddy and recent highwater marks are still visible. The water has the appearance and consistency of old crankcase oil. I figure I'm safe as long as I stay in the canoe.

Fortunately, we don't have to drink it. Yet. The thought occurs to me, though, that one day we might be refining this sludge and running it through our kitchen taps.

There are four of us on this trip. Frances and I are in one canoe. Bob Patenaude and his wife, Mary, are in another. Frances and Mary are down-hill skiing partners. Bob is a geophysicist. He has been to the Antarctic and he makes a fine home brew. Both are accomplishments I admire.

I think maybe we are a strange combination, the geophysicist and the scribe — one linked by profession to the ages, the other trying to make some sense of out of the present.

It is quiet on the river, as it should be. "Nature makes no noise," the great prophet Henry David Thoreau wrote. "The howling storm, the rustling leaf, the pattering rain are no disturbance, there is an essential and unexplored harmony in them."

Not far away, Interstate 90-94 is carrying thousands of weekend vacationers home to Illinois, home from way up north, from Woodruff and Tomahawk and Eagle River, from Ladysmith and Shell Lake and Spooner. The Baraboo River is not in tourist guidebooks. Down here on the river there is only us — and the turtles.

"Oh, look up there," says Mary, pointing to a single tree that houses four great blue heron nests. They are huge nests, loosely constructed from sticks and twigs, as awkward in appearance as the birds themselves.

Three of the birds leave their nests at our approach and fly over in large, watchful circles. The fourth stays put, only its head and neck visible from the river.

After a couple of hours of drifting on the Baraboo, the whine of boat motors warns us that we are nearing the Wisconsin, that we are about to re-enter the machine age.

Once into the Wisconsin, we beach the canoes on a wide clean sandbar and break out the lunches. There are sandwiches, apples, cheese, potato salad and a glass of Bob's homemade beer.

After lunch, we nap on the sand. A brisk breeze blowing across the river keeps us cool and bug-free.

For the rest of the afternoon, we drift down the wide Wisconsin. We see only a few motorboats and only one other flotilla of canoes. Near the end of the trip, we paddle into a slough and head back upstream to the pickup car, which we left in the tall grass at the end of a sandy road.

The interstate is still flooded with southbound traffic, bumper-to-bumper, hubcap-to-hubcap. We cross over it and take the back roads home, sometimes an adventure in itself.

There is, after all, no hurry. As another great prophet, Yogi Berra, said: "It ain't over 'til it's over."

A Snowshoe Jaunt

On a January morning, when the snow is piled in deep drifts where the wind had put it the night before, I go, on snowshoes, with a friend into the Wisconsin River bottomland near Mazomanie.

We are dressed warmly with chopper mitts and with wool stocking caps pulled down over our ears, but the bite of the cold is a presence we always feel, a presence that waits patiently for a bit of exposed skin upon which it clamps its icy grip before we can quickly cover it up again.

We walk along a trail that already is beginning to drift over. Then we set off through the unbroken snow, across a wide frozen marsh and into a patch of woods of largely poplar and pine. Mornings like this, except for the pounding of your own heart and the sound of your own breathing, are quiet, ethereal — a solitary dance on rawhide-webbed feet, staged on a field of white under a red glowing sun.

This is a world in which man is an intruder, a world that belongs to the field mouse in his maze of tunnels under the snow, to the foraging rabbit and the deer, to the owl waiting wide-eyed in the cold of night to pounce on any furry movement below.

I am quite content with my temporary residence here, content to sample for a moment the stark world of other creatures, to feel their cold and to sometimes sense the terror that must strike, however briefly, when a talon is thrust suddenly into a throbbing jugular.

This is not, I realize, for me. I am grateful now for my ancestors who developed the apposable thumb, who discovered fire and who invented the automobile, the hot shower, the reclining chair, Kentucky Fried Chicken.

This is my winter of 1985 and I am snug and comfortable in my cocoon of down and soft wool.

I remember other winters, too, the winters of the squeaking harness and the scrape of bobsled runner on snow, in which I was perhaps as warm but not nearly so comfortable; winters, stoically endured, in which November through March saw a one-piece suit of woolen underwear worn next to the skin, the winters of the violent itch.

These were the winters, too, of the slight stoop, because these one-piece garments had a tendency to shrink with each successive washing and I am convinced that man, even after eons of evolution, never really walked upright until he was suddenly released by the invention of two-piece underwear.

How I dreaded the Saturday night baths in those winters of the 1930s, in the washtub in front of the kitchen stove, knowing that when I finished and was dried I would have to pull on a clean pair of winter woollies, rough and tight and not yet broken in.

We all, it would seem, have our own private terrors to deal with.

We walk on, my friend and I, stopping occasionally to examine a track in the snow, to listen to the warning cry of a crow, a cry heard long before its ground-level shadow flies silently by.

How cold was it? It was so cold that when I moved my shadow stayed where it was, frozen fast to the ground.

This is the outdoor Wisconsin winter, in January, in the woods and the marshes and along the cold, icy river.

There is another winter I enjoy as much, if not more; the winter of the indoor quiet on a long lazy Saturday, the winter of the warm fire, the blazing log, the apple cider, the good book.

This is the winter I hurry to now. It is only a short drive away, in an automobile in which I can control the temperature inside.

"I think I like this," I say to my friend, "this modern winter of 1985." He nods in agreement.

I start the car and we wait, briefly, for the engine to begin to warm.

Hopkins making wood at the cabin.

Chapter Four

NOSTALGIA

Grandad's Old '51 Chevy

There is a joke about a salesman trying to sell a customer a used car that was owned by a little old lady who only took it out of the garage to drive to church on Sunday mornings.

Well, there is a 1951 Chevrolet parked in our driveway that for most of its years was treated about as well.

It first belonged to my wife's grandfather, in Wibaux, Montana, and much of its mileage was accumulated on short trips to the post office and back, a round trip of something like eight blocks.

In a way, they were a lot alike, the old man and the car, both humming along through the years, succumbing to time's relentless insistence only at the very end.

When both were younger, there were summer trips to Yellowstone at the other end of the state and an occasional trip to Minneapolis, some 600 miles away, and back.

In later years, most of the trips were only downtown, to the post office, or to the Stockman's Bar where the old man would park the car in the alley and go in through the back door for a game or two of rummy with some of his old friends, most of them retired cattlemen.

Wibaux is an eastern Montana prairie town of about 700, named after a French cattleman, Pierre Wibaux, who was one of the early settlers.

My wife's grandfather, a Minneapolis-area native, got off the train there one night when he was a young man and decided to stay. He was a butcher by trade. He later became a rancher, an implement dealer and, eventually, a retired gentleman.

My wife was raised there, by her grandparents, and, when she was a young bride, took me home with her one summer. We returned many summers, and our children came to know Wibaux, and all of them knew their great-grandparents.

But on that first trip in that first summer, my wife and I and her grandparents all piled in the car, known affectionately in the family as "the 51," and headed for a tour of the Wibaux County oil fields.

There are not a lot of side roads in eastern Montana, and often, when the destination is not along the main road, the driver will simply drive off the road and head out across the open prairie. It comes as a bit of a shock to the uninitiated. This trip was like that.

Grandad and I sat in the front seat, Frances and her grandmother in the back.

Grandad chewed cigars, and, consequently, since it was a hot day and all the car windows were open, when he would spit out the front window some of it would reenter the car through the back window.

"Oh Fred," Grandma would say, "throw that nasty thing away." And Grandad would just clamp down a little tighter on his cigar, step a little harder on the accelerator and continue to bounce along through the prairie grass. Grandma would roll up the car window; Grandad would chuckle softly to himself.

By the time they put the interstate highway around Wibaux, he was a little too old to comprehend its intricacies.

Grandad liked good rich cream in his coffee and on his berries, the kind that is so thick it has to be spooned from the jar. There was a farm just out of town, and he would make a weekly trip there to buy it.

One morning I went with him. The farm lane was only a few yards from the interstate exit, and, on this particular morning, he turned too soon, and, before we knew it, we were heading up the interstate the wrong way. We both were a little shaken by the time we got turned around and back on the right path.

My last trip in the car with him was a few years ago when my son, Peter, was 9. Grandad, who had not fished for years, decided to take his great-grandson bullhead fishing on Beaver Creek.

Everything had to be done just right. The new spinning rods I had with me would not do. Grandad cut three willow sticks, one for each of us, and rigged them up with fishing line, bobbers, sinkers and hooks. I forget what we used for bait, but I think it must have been worms.

We drove out into the country and down a dirt road until he pulled off and parked under a clump of willows beside the stream. The rear wheels sank into the sand.

We caught a mess of bullheads from his favorite hole. He caught some of them himself, but mostly he sat in the shade of an old willow watching his great-grandson fish. He would offer an occasional piece of advice, and he patiently taught Peter the fine art of removing a wriggling bullhead from a fishhook.

When the afternoon was over and we returned to the car, the wheels had sunk even deeper into the sand.

Now the old man, who had never offered to let me drive before, looked at me with a mischievous gleam in his eye: "I'll never get it out of there," he said. "You drive."

On the way home, he seemed deep in thought. Finally, he turned to me and said: "I guess that was my last fishing trip." It turned out that it was.

He died the following year, and Frances drove the old car back to Madison. For eight years, it served us well as a second car. It was as reliable and dependable as the old man, and, often, on cold winter mornings, it would start when the other car wouldn't and take us where we had to go. Peter learned to drive in it.

I remember one day I drove it, rattling and banging, into a service station and pulled up alongside a young woman who was driving a Corvette.

The Corvette was shiny and new, and the old 51 even then was beginning to show signs of rust and wear. The young woman was dressed in her finest. I was dressed in some tattered old fishing clothes.

"I see we both have Chevies," I said, "how do you like yours?" She gave me a look of utter disgust and then turned haughtily away.

The old 51 has been all but retired now, and a new car stands behind it in the driveway. We still use it once in awhile — for a short trip to the post office or the drugstore, but it's showing its age, and its parts are beginning to wear out.

This summer I might take it on one last fishing trip, not a long trip — maybe just down to Mt. Vernon Creek.

I think the old car, if it could remember, would like that. I know Grandad would.

Sentimental Journey

I got a notice in the mail last week reminding me that my 30th high school class reunion is coming up this summer.

I dug my high school yearbook from its place on the top bookshelf and blew the dust from the cover. I opened it and there I was, 30 years ago — a skinny kid with a full head of hair. The class prophecy predicted I would be a barber and I was, for awhile.

When I thought about it, 1947 seemed a long time ago.

How do you measure 30 years?

I suppose you can measure it by the things you've done, and when I think of it that way, it all seems to have happened pretty fast.

I spent three years of it working at odd jobs, four years of it in the Air Force, another four years of it at the university and nearly 20 years of it writing for The State Journal.

I've been married for more than 20 years, and we have raised a family. I've owned two houses and 14 cars. I've lost nearly all of my hair. I've saved almost no money.

Maybe you can measure 30 years by changes in a society.

I've seen places change. I've seen cities grow and small towns shrivel and die.

Madison was just beginning to grow in 1947. The west city limit sign was halfway down Nakoma hill then, and there was a farm there. What now is Midvale Blvd. and everything west of it, where I live now, was country.

There were no three-bedroom ranches, no supermarkets and no shopping centers, only a few neighborhood grocery stores.

Fashions changed. Men wore sport coats then with the shirt collars on the outside, and I have noticed recently that they are wearing them that way again. The most popular hair style was the crew cut.

Women wore their hair in pageboy bobs, and they wore bobby sox and pleated plaid skirts that swirled around their legs when they walked.

People listened to Frank Sinatra and Tony Bennett and Dick Haymes and to Helen O'Connell and Jo Stafford and Doris Day. They danced to the music of Les Brown and Harry James and Benny Goodman and to Tommy and Jimmy Dorsey and Artie Shaw.

One of the biggest changes in the last 30 years has been in music. Some of us older folks have suffered through years of ear-splitting hard rock, but now some of the old music is coming back.

One night just a few years ago, during the hard rock era, my wife and I were at Disneyland, in California. We heard familiar music through the noise of the crowd, and we followed it to an open-air dance pavilion where Les Brown and his orchestra were playing.

There were only a handful of couples dancing, and my wife and I joined them. We danced over to Les Brown, and I said, "I remember you."

He looked at us, a middle-aged couple holding each other on a dance floor, and he said, "I remember you, too."

When that song was over, he turned and said something to the band, and they swung into "Sentimental Journey."

For years I heard only electric guitars coming from the stereo in my son's room. Only a few days ago I heard a new sound coming from his room, one of my old records — the Bobby Hackett trumpet riding softly on "Blue Turning Grey Over You."

It was good to see Frank Sinatra and Tony Bennett on television again the other night. They've changed a little through the years. Frank is grayer and Tony wears glasses, but the old magnetism still is there.

"Listen to them," I told my oldest daughter, Katy. "They're still the best there is."

The society we know today just began to emerge about 1947, an off-shoot of the technology and mass production techniques developed during World War II.

There had been a great depression and there had been long hard years of war that had called for sacrifice, both on the battlefield and on the home front.

Now there was peace and a booming economy. We went on a nation-wide spree.

There have been two other wars since, one of which nearly destroyed the country, but neither called for sacrifices on the home front. It's been a long time since we have felt a necessity to sacrifice.

We became the world's greatest consumers. We attacked the land and our resources like a plague of locusts.

"We want more," we said. "More! More! More!"

Earlier this year, during a bitter cold January, furnaces went out in homes and industries around the nation. We began to talk about an energy crisis. Some even took it seriously.

Now the President speaks to Congress and to a nation of people, and he calls the energy crisis the "moral equivalent of war." He asks us to make sacrifices and changes in our lives.

Can we?

Will we?

History probably will measure the years between 1947 and 1977 as the length of time it took to suck the Earth nearly dry.

But the last 30 years have been good to me, and I remember them fondly.

We are a nation of good people, and we have done some things right and some things wrong. We have been misguided and misdirected, perhaps, but we never were evil. We just didn't know.

One thing I have learned in the last 30 years is that we are, after all, only human.

The years around 1947 were good years. If the low-energy lifestyle we have been asked to adopt means a return to 1947 values and standards, I'm all for it.

Life, as I remember it, was less hectic then, but we had everything we needed.

In some ways, we're headed in that direction now. Trends in fashion and music already have started to reverse.

And I kind of like Les Brown.

No apology

We ran a photograph in this newspaper not long ago of a scene from a picturesque Wisconsin college town.

A couple of days later, we received a letter from a resident of that community.

"We were pleased to see the picture," he wrote, "but it was followed by a caption stating that this is a 'small community.'

"What is meant by 'small' anyhow?" he asked. "It seems to me that this is a demeaning term."

He pointed out that the population is 4,759, that it is the fastest-growing city in its county, that it has four brand new school buildings.

"We are proud of our city and its accomplishments," he wrote, "and do not relish demeaning language."

I am taking the opportunity to reply to his letter in this column:

Dear Sir:

I read your letter, and I wonder what is happening to America and to Americans.

We once were proud of our rural communities. They were and still are, as far as I know, the backbone of this country, the kind of places where everybody either came from or lives in now or hopes to live in someday. Where, along the way, did we get the idea that bigger is better?

Your particular town, as I remember it, is kind of special. It combines all the best qualities of the small community.

I could understand your reaction had we called it a "hick town" or even a "sleepy little hamlet," but "small" simply is not a derogatory word.

It could be, of course, that you know your community better than I do. If people now pass each other on the streets without exchanging a friendly "Hello," then you are right. Yours no longer is a small town.

Perhaps, since I was last there, the numbers of muggings and robberies have increased and your community now claims the fastest-growing crime rate in the county. That certainly would help qualify it for big-city status.

I sincerely hope none of this has happened.

I realize there are many of us who have fond memories of small towns and would like them to remain the way we remember them. This, I know, can't be because change is inevitable. But I do hope it is possible for a small town to grow and build new schools, and still retain the rural characteristics that attracted the new people in the first place.

My definition of a small town apparently is quite different from yours.

A small town to me, you see, is a place where people really know and care about each other; a place where you are never alone when you need friends.

It is the kind of place where you can leave your house unlocked at night, where you can park your car and leave your keys in it — and it will still be there when you return.

A small town is a true community where everyone feels a responsibility for everyone else and where even a stray dog is never without a friendly pat, a leftover bone or a rug on somebody's porch to spend the night on.

It is the kind of place where your daughter can walk safely alone at night.

A small town is shady, tree-lined streets and big, old two-story houses.

It is the corner drugstore; it is an ancient wooden church with its steeple piercing the sky.

It is the smell of leaves burning on an autumn evening. It is homecoming bonfires and Memorial Day parades and high school proms and Sunday afternoon band concerts in the park.

It is a friendly place where the baldest man is called "Curly," the tallest man is known as "Shorty" and where there are several men who answer to the nickname of "Doc."

A small town, to a nation of city youngsters, is a place where grandmas and grandpas live.

And a small town, I'm proud to be able to say, is the kind of place in which I once lived.

So you see, sir, I don't consider the term "small town" at all demeaning but, rather, a compliment of the highest order.

Therefore, no apology will be forthcoming.

Sincerely,

Steve Hopkins.

A pot-bellied stove for everyone

Within the circle of men with whom I fish and sometimes hunt I am considered a youngster.

But there are times when I feel old.

It happens when I am talking with a group of people and suddenly discover I am the only one who remembers certain things, like the "Quarantine" signs that used to be hung on the front door when somebody in the house had come down with measles or scarlet fever.

This comes to mind because it is the New Year and, by accident of birth and through no doing of my own, it happens to be my 48th time around.

There have been a lot of changes, some of them good, but most of the progress, it seems to me, has been at considerable cost. A way of life has been lost, and now that I think back on it that way of life might have been the low-energy lifestyle many of us now are so urgently seeking.

We heated with wood and coal back in the early years and now we are heating with wood again and enjoying it.

Show me someone who spent the winters of his youth warming up by a kitchen range, with his mittens drying on an open oven door, and does not now cherish that memory.

Show me someone who does not remember fondly the taste of cold pure well water, the smell of wool drying in front of a fire, the sharp metallic smell of a cold sled runner, the tart taste of a winter apple, the sound of a Model-T engine, an evening with Fibber McGee and Molly around the big parlor stove.

There were some problems then, most of them, as I remember, economic, but we endured, and in the end we were stronger because of it.

Television had not yet come along to occupy our time and attention and we made our own entertainment. There were card games and dice games and bingo games around the kitchen table.

And I remember quilting parties, with the women seated around a rectangular quilting frame, talking and laughing as they sewed.

But the gatherings I remember most fondly were the gatherings of men — in the gas stations, around the pot-bellied stove in the lumberyard office, around the coal stove in the depot, and in the barber shop.

The depot had its own smell, of warm tar or creosote, and there was something comforting in the sound of the constantly clicking telegraph key. The lumberyard smelled of fresh wood, and the flames in the stove there burned more brightly than anywhere else because of the constant feeding of shavings and waste ends of pine.

Because my father was a barber, I suppose I spent more than my share of time in a barber shop. And my early education was gleaned from the conversations of men waiting their turns for shaves and haircuts — the shop keepers, the livestock dealer, the Lutheran minister and the Catholic priest, the feed dealer, the lumberman, the doctor, the dentist and the farmers.

There do not seem to be, at least in the city, places where men gather anymore to talk; unless you count the taverns and I have found that any attempt at conversation there tends to deteriorate in a very short time.

The barber shop smelled of a mixture of exotic preparations: Lucky Tiger and Wildroot tonics, Southern Rose hair oil, Sweet Pea and Lilac after shave lotions, Witch Hazel and Bay Rum, and Fitch and pine-tar shampoos. Many of the customers were farmers, and when they came in and thawed out by the stove they often added a touch of the cow barn to the overall aroma.

The shave was a thing of beauty to behold — the application of the hot steam towels to soften the beard, the careful lathering, the stropping of the straight-edge razor, the smooth graceful strokes that separated the beard from the face, and the almost surgical skill involved in shaving the upper lip at the exact point where it joins the nose.

Boys, in those days, spent a lot of time watching and observing and learning. And I have watched my share of shaves and haircuts, of boxcar loadings and steam engine waterings, of oil changes and tire changes, of cheesemaking and buttermaking, of harness making and horse shoeing — and I did it all within a block or two of Main Street in one small Dane County town.

If I were to make a New Year's resolution, it would be to strive to restore some of this way of life — and I think I would start by putting a pot-bellied stove in every supermarket and in every shopping center mall.

Wouldn't we be pleasantly surprised if, when we gathered around it, we found the warmth we were seeking not only in the stove, but also again in each other?

Railroad Days

The railroad train has all but disappeared from the American scene and, with it, a way of life that probably never will return.

To a boy growing up in Mt. Horeb in the '30s, their noisy comings and goings were a constant source of curiosity. What exotic cargoes did they carry? What adventures would they bring?

And what boy could help but idolize the men who ran them: the engineer with the peaked polka-dot cap, shiny gold watch and colorful red bandana who leaned out of the window and smiled and waved as he sped past; the brakeman who hung by one arm from the platform at the back of the caboose, his swinging red lantern spreading a glowing path through the night.

Ours was the second house coming into town from the West. It was a small, two-story frame house with a back porch that looked out, past the pump in the yard and across a small garden, to the railroad tracks less than a hundred yards away.

The trains would begin to slow down here as they approached the first crossing and the depot only a short distance up the tracks. The steam whistles, warning of their approach, could be heard while they still were a long way out of town. I still can hear the whistles sometimes in my mind at night.

Back in the Depression years, the freights brought all manner of unexpected visitors, the restless, unemployed men of the '30s. They were politely called hobos, although some called them tramps and some called them bums.

We could see them drop off the train when it slowed, and we would watch them approach the house and finally knock on the screen door.

"Got something to eat, M'am?" they would say to my mother. "I'm willing to work for it."

We turned few, if any, away. They would be put to work at the woodpile or at the lawn mower while my mother busied herself making sandwiches in the kitchen.

Their visits were not unwelcomed by a small boy who otherwise would have had to perform these chores himself. I would sit and watch them work, listening in fascination to the tales of adventure some of them had to tell.

I was among the most privileged of young men. Our next-door neighbor, Conrad Wagner, who is gone now, was the section crew foreman. He knew all the trainmen, and I often would be with him when he talked to them.

I was not yet six-years-old when I first was shown into the cab of a steam engine and allowed to look into the firebox. I'm told I ran away crying and screaming.

Later, on infrequent occasions, I was allowed to board the caboose, where I would sit by the small glowing pot-bellied stove and ride the short distance to the depot.

Conrad patroled the tracks every day on a small handcar and sometimes would let me ride on it with him. Keeping some 20 miles of track in order in the heat of summer and intense cold of winter was a job for an extremely hardy man — and that he was.

The callouses on his hands were so thick he could grind out a lighted cigaret on his palm. Yet I never knew a more gentle man.

He was an unofficial neighborhood physician and veterinarian. Those same rough hands gently would bandage a cut finger or a scraped knee, and many an injured bird or animal benefited from his tender care. He kept goldfish in a rock garden in his yard. He had a way with flowers and all growing things.

The summer after I was out of high school, I went to work for him and learned how to drive spikes, tamp sand under ties and cut bull thistles with a scythe. I got to drive the handcar.

I remember my first day of hard labor under a burning summer sun. The other members of the crew were grizzled old tobacco-chewing men. The only water supply was a wooden barrel with a dipper in it. A layer of tobacco juice floated on top of the water, and I vowed I would not drink.

Finally, when I could stand the thirst no longer, I walked to the barrel, shoved the dipper to the bottom and brought it up quickly. Most of the tobacco juice ran off the outside of the dipper. I drank greedily. The old men smiled. I had passed the test. And I have not been a finicky eater since.

Conrad was a member of a long-time railroading family. His brother, Fred, also gone now, was the depot master, and I still can see him sitting at the telegraph key by the big window in the depot, his pet bulldog curled up on the counter beside him.

The depot was the center of activity in the community in those days; the town literally had sprung up around it.

The freights picked up milk and baked goods which were produced at the local bakery for sale in other towns. On Mondays, it stopped at the stockyards to pick up cattle for the market.

There was a passenger train, too, known locally as the "Toonerville Trolley," and shoppers even could go to Madison or Milwaukee and be back in the same day.

There was a waiting room in the depot with a big wood-burning stove and wooden benches and a big blackboard with the train schedules chalked in. The schedules never changed and people in town knew them by heart.

There was a big old water tower to climb, and there always were empty freight cars on the sidetrack by the stockyard. As boys, we would climb the iron rungs on the side and pretend we were trainmen, racing across the narrow platform on the top and leaping daringly from one car to another. It probably was not allowed, but I don't remember that Fred ever stopped us. I think he understood.

Then one day, I don't remember just when, the depot was shut down, and the trains didn't stop there anymore.

People said trucks were more efficient and more economical.

More and more trucks began to roar down Main Street, leaving clouds of foul blue smoke in their wakes. The train whistle was replaced by the noisy honking of horns.

The trucks had stickers on their windshields that warned: "No Hitchhikers."

The truck drivers wore strained expressions on their faces, and they looked straight ahead, cigarets dangling from the corners of their mouths.

They didn't smile. And they never waved.

Who'll remind us?

There are people around, born near the turn of the century, who have witnessed most of the changes that have taken place in the world. They are the people who remember when times were different — when there were no automobiles, no television, no central heating or air conditioning, no electricity, no telephones and no indoor plumbing.

They will agree that living was more difficult then, but they are proud of having lived in those days, and they remember them fondly. Few will agree that life today, with all of our technological advances, is better.

I sometimes wonder what the world will be like when these people are gone, when they no longer are around to remind us of the way things were; when the only people left are those who were born after 1950, people whose only memories are of supermarkets, self-service gas stations and drive-in restaurants — people who remember only affluence and the good life.

I happened to have been born somewhere in the middle, but maybe, for my taste, just a bit too late. I remember a lot about the way things were, but I missed a lot of it, too, and, sometimes, in the company of older folks, I feel a little left out.

I missed the old general stores with the cracker barrel seats and the pot-bellied stoves.

I always am saddened and more than a little envious when an older fishing companion of mine says, "The trout fishing isn't what it was 20 years ago. There were some real fish in the streams then."

I wish I had been able to hunt during the time when huge migrating flocks of ducks and geese took days and nights to pass overhead.

But I suppose what I miss most is a way of life in which a simple thing like buying a pouch of pipe tobacco was a pleasant event that involved more than an exchange of money.

I'm referring to the old independently-owned stores and shops presided over by gentlemen who were both proprietor and friend.

There are some left, mostly in the rural areas, but they are few and far between.

There is a drugstore in a small town I visit frequently when I am in northern Wisconsin. I felt at home there the first time I walked in, and I soon came to know the old pharmacist well.

The store was housed in an ancient two-story, wood-frame building on the town's main street, and, the first time I saw it, the building already was beginning to sag and seemed only still to be standing because it was leaning against a newer, sturdier brick building next door.

The pharmacist, too, seemed to rely similarly on his high, old-fashioned prescription counter for support. They were a lot alike, the old man and the building.

The store was comfortable and cluttered, the way a drugstore ought to be, and the top shelves were gathering dust that probably dated back to the days the old man gave up climbing stepladders. But somewhere, in the midst of all the clutter, was everything you would expect to find in a drugstore.

The old pharmacist opened the store every day about 6 a.m., sometimes a few minutes earlier, but never later.

He walked from his home a few blocks away with his dog, which accompanied him everywhere he went, at his side.

He would turn the key in the latch, bend to pick up the bundle of newspapers in the doorway, shove the door open with his shoulder and walk inside.

Then he would shuffle to the back of the store behind the prescription counter, where he would, in the colder months, fire up the oil space heater. The dog would curl up on a rug by the stove, the pharmacist would turn to his work and the store was open for business.

The old man was quite a talker, and he liked to talk about the old days when he was young and when the town was young and filled with youth and life.

Once a Boy Scout leader, he still received cards and letters from former Scouts, all of whom had grown up and now lived in other cities and other towns. He kept these in a drawer, in an old roll-top desk.

He had been quite a hunter and quite a fisherman, and when he talked about these things the old dog's ears would pick up and the tip of his tail would wag, just a little. I suspect they talked to each other, often, when there was no one else in the store.

We seem to have to have reasons for doing things, so I used to look for excuses to stop at the store when I was in town. Sometimes it would be to pick up a morning paper, sometimes a magazine, sometimes pipe tobacco or a package of razor blades.

I always felt better when I left than I had before I went in.

One day, I parked in front of the store under a new sign that announced it now was part of a drugstore chain.

There was carpeting on the floor, and the shelves had been dusted and restacked. Everything was neat and orderly, and there was the faint smell of perfume in the air. A prim, middle-aged woman, a stranger, stood behind a new computerized cash register at the tobacco counter.

I looked to the back of the room. The old prescription counter and the space heater were gone. There was no sign of the old man or his dog.

I bought a newspaper and waited while she rang up the sale amid a flurry of electronic bleeps and buzzings and blurps. My change rolled down a chute and spilled into a metal tray, a classic example of modern merchandising theory: "Don't touch the customer; you never know where he's been."

I picked up my change. "What happened to the old pharmacist who used to be here?" I asked.

"I don't know," she answered. "I haven't been here long."

Aging gratefully

There is one major difference between this and all of the other columns I have written over the years:

This is the first column written by a 50-year-old man.

I don't feel that old. My mother still calls me Stevie.

The main reaction I have to reaching the half-century mark is that I don't feel any different at all.

My favorite comment about aging, and I don't remember where I read it or who said it, went something like this: "When I was 50, I found I no longer could do the things I could when I was 20, but I didn't care because I didn't want to do them anyway. But, at 70, I wish I still could do the things I could when I was 50."

When you get right down to it, 50 is kind of a nice age — if you're lucky and in relatively good health.

I suppose the best thing about it (and I've felt it coming on for a few years now) is that I no longer have to prove anything to anybody. I am free of the pressures of youth, the pressure to succeed — or at least the pressure to appear successful.

I can wear baggy old clothes and sweaters with holes in the elbows, and nobody notices or cares. There is no pressure to drive a new car. My rusty old truck and I get along fine; we understand each other.

There is no pressure to run faster or drink harder than the other guy. I can wink at a pretty girl without getting my face slapped.

I am skiing better then ever this winter, but there is no need for the Olympic stars to begin looking over their shoulders. I am becoming a better trout fisherman, probably because I am far less impatient than in earlier years.

I am reminded of the old fellow who, when asked what he would do differently if he could live his life over, said, "I'd do exactly the same thing, except I would start a lot sooner."

There is not much I would change if I could do it over, and I wouldn't do it over if I could.

Many people don't realize this, but a lot of effort goes into becoming a 50-year-old man; there are almost insurmountable obstacles to overcome.

You know what I remember about being young?

I remember being a small, skinny kid in grade school and standing in the schoolyard while two bigger kids chose up sides for softball — and waiting and waiting for my name to be called. It does something to you, when you're chosen last, and you remember it for a long, long time.

I remember being a little, but not much, bigger in high school and making the football team — as a third-string quarterback.

A third-string quarterback seldom plays, except in practice, and I remember a game in which the first-string quarterback was injured and was taken out; then the second-string quarterback was injured and left the field.

It was my big chance. "Hopkins," the coach yelled. I reached for my helmet. "Run over to the school bus," he said, "and get my overcoat." I looked around on my way to the bus in time to see the first-string quarterback limp back onto the field.

I remember what it's like to have pimples and finally getting up the nerve to ask a girl to the high school prom — and having her laugh in my face.

It hurts sometimes, to be young.

I kind of like things the way they are now. My complexion has cleared up, and my wife doesn't laugh at me.

I think, as you approach 50, people stop trying to change or improve you.

Old Tom Alberti has patiently taught me much of what I know about fishing, but he didn't abandon me when I failed to measure up. And one day a couple of years ago he paid me what for him was the extreme compliment: "Hopkins," he said, "you aren't much of a fisherman, but you certainly are the most enthusiastic fisherman I know."

At 50, people begin to accept you for what you are.

Even my wife is growing more tolerant of me. My flyrod, all rigged up, still leans against the fireplace in the living room in the exact same spot I left it on the last day of the season last summer. Not once has she suggested I take it to the basement.

I ask the kids about my skiing form, and they tell me, "You do fine — for an old man."

Sometimes I think I have been 50 for most of my life, and, now that I'm finally here, I feel comfortable with it. It seems to suit my personality.

The world, viewed through trifocals, still looks good, and I find I still can do almost everything I always did — I just grunt more.

Good Old Days at Gas Station

There was a Cities Service gas station in the town I grew up in during the 1930s.

It was a small square building with a steep peaked roof. It sat right at the edge of town, separated from the last house by a vacant lot that was used largely for neighborhood softball games.

Oil changes were done outside, on an old-fashioned grease rack, the kind you carefully drove your car up and onto.

Youngsters played on it between oil changes. It was a versatile grease rack. It would serve as a fort one day and a battleship the next.

There weren't many cars then. You could sit on your front porch at night, right on the main highway, and count the ones that went by. On a busy night you might get all the way up to 10.

Life was just a little easier then, a little slower and maybe just a little nicer.

There was a soda pop cooler in the gas station and you could lift up the lid and the bottles sat half-submerged in ice water. You read the flavors from the caps — Nehi Orange, Orange Crush, Coca-Cola, White Soda, Root Beer, Cream Soda.

You picked out a bottle, snapped off the cap on the opener beside the cooler and then laid a nickel down by the cash register, on a glass counter top that was so scratched and clouded by use you could barely see through it anymore.

The gas station was one of the town gathering places and men would come in to sit and play a little cards, but mostly just to find somebody to talk to.

The characters changed from time to time, but the conversation seldom did. The same conversation went on and on, like a soap opera, and you could walk in and pick it up at any time of the day or week without missing anything.

This was a farming community and the topics usually were politics and farming. The crops were aways bad. It was either too wet or too dry. Either way, it was the government's fault.

There was, of course, talk about the Depression, and, toward the end of the decade, words like "war" and "Hitler" began to creep into the conversations. They were strange and frightening words to the ears of a 9 or 10-year-old boy.

Saturday night was the big night in town and the stores were open until midnight. There always was a dance in the town dance hall. There was a popcorn stand on the sidewalk on Main Street, and the movie theater was going full blast.

Everybody came to town, from miles around. And they visited in the stores and in doorways and on the streets and in the taverns and barbershops and even in the cars parked along Main Street.

The trick, if you lived in town, was to park your car on Main Street in the afternoon and then walk home for supper. Then you would walk back after supper and sit in your car. You could see everyone who went past, and most would stop to talk awhile through the car window.

It would take hours to walk down Main Street because you had to stop and visit with everyone you met. There was always plenty to talk and gossip about. And there were frequent outbursts of laughter.

The war did come along and when it was over the Depression had ended, too. Times were good. Everybody had jobs. Everybody had money. Everybody had cars. A way of life was nearing an end.

The gas station operator built an addition and installed a modern grease rack. He was busy with oil changes and tune-ups now. Too busy to talk and play cards.

The young merchants and businessmen no longer wanted to work on Saturday nights, so they began closing early. The people had discovered television and Perry Como and Jackie Gleason, and they didn't really care. The movie theater shut down.

Shoppers began driving through town, in one end and out the other, headed for the city where there were the beginnings of supermarkets and shopping centers and the highest standard of living the world has ever known.

You could have stopped them then, I suppose, and said: "Listen! Do you know what you're doing? You're destroying your town! You're abandoning a way of life. Don't you know there are values that can't be measured in dollars and cents?"

They wouldn't have listened. They wouldn't have cared. "Things are cheaper there," they would have said. "There is a better selection."

The old town is still there, but it has changed and it is not at all the same.

You can go to a city shopping center on a Sunday afternoon now, and, if you can find a parking place, you can go inside and you will see crowds of shoppers, carrying bags loaded with cheap polyester clothing and gadgets. They scurry, like mice, from store to store and from bargain to bargain, greedily buying things they will never need or use.

If you look closely, you will see those who have come there to seek, in their own ways, some kind of social life, some kind of sense of community.

Often, these are older people with memories of gas stations and barbershops and small town Saturday nights.

Now they sit, among strangers, on plastic chairs in the lounge areas of shopping center malls.

They listen to the piped-in music and to the bargains being announced over the speaker system.

They look at the fountains and the plastic flowers and the artificial waterfalls, and they watch the shoppers hurrying by. They stare blankly at each other.

They seldom speak.

And they never laugh.

Music and the Way We Were

A couple of nights ago my youngest daughter, Jayne, called me from the university at Whitewater where she is a student and said she had to know a few things about Benny Goodman and the Big Band Era.

It was, she said, some information she needed for an English course.

"You are talking to the right man," I told her. "Just what is it you want to know?"

"When," she asked, "did the Big Band Era end?"

"Well, that's not something you can put a date on like it was the Declaration of Independence or something," I answered. "The Big Band Era never really ended, it just kind of faded away.

"What we know as the Big Band Era probably started sometime in the late '20s, and grew through the '30s and the World War II years of the early '40s; then began to wind down sometime near the end of the '40s."

"Why?" she asked.

"Who knows?" I answered. "Things change. Public tastes change. We had just gone through a depression and major war. Maybe the nation that emerged was taking itself more seriously. It seemed to somehow quit dancing for awhile.

"And the musicians were changing, too. Many of the same ones were there, but they were breaking up into smaller groups, experimenting with different music like modern jazz.

"The big band was replaced with progressive jazz trios and quartets and quintets, and by popular vocalists with small backup groups."

We talked some more about music and about Benny Goodman, who certainly was and still is a big part of it, and before we hung up I said, "Jayne, those were wonderful years, great years. I wish you could have been there."

Thinking it over later, it occurred to me that as we grow older we abandon most of what was familiar in our youth and we adapt to a world that keeps changing around us.

Our priorities change. Our interests change. Often our values change. It is only our music that we take with us forever.

And those among us who ever wore saddle shoes and danced in a high school gym to the music of the Glenn Miller Orchestra will remember "In the Mood" for the rest of our lives, and we will feel a familiar stirring whenever we hear it.

I suppose it is possible for someone from another generation to feel the same way about The Beach Boys, The Rolling Stones and even (Ugh!) The Grateful Dead.

I'm not a musical snob. I love a good old-fashioned polka band. I have spent a small fortune in roadhouse jukeboxes throughout the north woods, punching up such country and western classics as "Good Hearted Woman" (one of my favorites), "Mammas, Don't Let Your Babies Grow Up to be Cowboys," and "Put Your Sweet Lips a Little Closer to the Phone."

I heard another one the other night that is destined, I think, to become a classic. It is called, "I Stepped into a Pile of You and Got Love All Over Me."

This is good foot-stomping and beer-drinking music but it does not endure. Kenny Rogers, sooner or later, will have to clear his throat. Willie Nelson is not Hoagy Carmichael and Loretta (if you ain't Country, you ain't nothin') Lynn certainly is not Anita O'Day. Guitar plucking and nasal twanging can wear a little thin. Country stars shine briefly; then quickly dim. Nashville is harder on cowboys than piranhas on Amazon fishermen.

But country and rock did come along and for a time they drowned out everything else in an ear-splitting, electronically amplified din. Music became one, long, repetitious screech. The radio stations were about evenly divided between rock and country.

Those of us who enjoyed the big bands, the standards, were suddenly out in the cold. We knew all the words to songs nobody played anymore. We were left with only our record collections and our memories.

There were a few bright spots. We could follow jazz trumpeter Doc DeHaven around Madison and hear music the way it ought to be played. There were and still are some nice modern jazz groups playing in some of the clubs.

There is a radio station out of Sun Prairie that features "The Music of Your Life."

Three of its hosts are quite probably the Madison area's best-known music men: Jim Mader (J.M. in the a.m.), Clark Hogan (Clark until dark) and George Vukelich (alias Papa Hambone, alias Billy P.). It is not unlike having Bart Starr, Joe Namath and John Unitas on the same team.

And, if you listen to them long enough, you will hear all the big bands, every standard ever recorded, all the music you ever danced to on a soft spring night, under a blue crepe paper sky with a yellow cardboard moon dangling dizzily overhead.

We cling to our music because the world of our music is a world in which nothing changes, it is a world in which Perry Como is always 30 years old, a world in which Nat King Cole remains forever alive.

Our music is the way we were. We cling to it because it is young love, because it is lost dreams, because it is, in the end, all we have left of our youth.

Hopkins in the Brule River.

Chapter Five

QUIET PEOPLE. QUIET PLACES.

No Returning to the Sea

There is a little community in New Brunswick, on the Bay of Fundy, called Alma.

It was named after a British victory in the Crimean War. Some of the few who live there now make their living catering to the tourists who come in the summer to nearby Fundy National Park, but most of its residents are fishermen.

When you first see Alma, you have the feeling you've seen it before because it looks like every calendar picture or National Geographic photo you've ever seen of a North Atlantic fishing village.

When the tide is in, the water covers the beach and fills an estuary that is located almost in the center of town. When the tide is out, there is about a half a mile of beach, and the estuary is muddy basin with only a small stream trickling down through the center of it on its way to the sea.

The fishermen have to time their trips, because they can only go in and out on the tide.

They earn their livings from the sea, but they do not live in it and, when they have harvested its crop, they return each night to homes which cling tenaciously to the rocky coast at the very edge of the land.

Life here, with certain concessions to the environment, is much the same as it is inland.

When you walk along the beach, following the tide as it goes out, you always are accompanied by seagulls.

If you stand on the beach and look inland, you see only the rugged wooded hills of New Brunswick, and you know something of what the early explorers must have felt when they first approached the coastline of the North American continent.

If you look out over the bay you see only open water. On a clear day you can see the blue outline of Nova Scotia, but, beyond that, there is only the open sea.

There is a small, neat, weathered frame cottage with a fresh coat of blue paint that sits on a point that juts out into the bay.

We rented it this summer from a trim, neatly dressed woman who greeted us at the door of her own home, peering at us through a pair of spectacles which, when not in use, dangled from a gold chain around her neck.

She showed us around, turned over the key and informed us, in her best New Brunswick dialect: "If you be wanting anything, stop at the house. I be home most of the day."

There is a picture window in the cottage that looks out over the bay and to get to the bay from the cottage you have to cross a wooden bridge over a small stream and follow a narrow winding path through an area of sand dunes.

We spent the days and some of the nights wandering up and down the beach. There seems always to be a wind and sometimes at night a heavy fog rolls in from the bay and covers the village. That is when you really feel alone in the world, when you can hear the sea but cannot see it.

At one end of the beach there is a steep rocky cliff to climb. It is not particularly dangerous because there are wide hand and footholds, but it is straight up and down and, when you are clinging to a rock near the top and look down, you see only the water and the spray from the waves that are crashing into the rocks at the foot of the cliff.

One day we drove along the coast on a little-used gravel road looking for a point identified on a map as Cape Enrage. There is a lighthouse on the cape and a small white cottage and a boathouse. Standing on the tip of the cape and looking down into the water it's easy to imagine how it looks during a storm and how it got its name.

On the way back we passed a wide, flat area that looked like a bright green meadow. There was a couple walking around there, carrying baskets. We stopped the car and walked out to talk to them.

They were an elderly couple from the nearby coastal community of Hillsborough. Both had the lean, sparse look that you come to identify with people who live simply, close to the land.

"Is this what is called a salt marsh?" I asked.

"Aye," he answered pleasantly.

I was full of questions about tides and here was a man who could answer them. He did, willingly. He answered questions about the salt marshes and the estuaries and the high tides and the low tides and the coastal storms.

Finally, I pointed to the wide stretch of sandy and rocky area between the marsh and the bay. "Then that area out there would be a tide flat?" I asked.

"I suppose you could call it that," he smiled, indulgently, "but mostly we just call it the beach."

They were, it turned out, picking an edible salt marsh plant called goose tongue greens much in the way that people in the Midwest go out and search for watercress.

They gave us some to sample and we picked some ourselves. Goose tongue greens, when boiled, have a slightly strong, distinctive flavor and it would be easy to develop a taste for them.

One evening, when the tide was out, I walked to the edge of the water and sat for a long time in the sand in the lee of a huge driftwood log, the land on one side of me and the sea on the other.

I had come to the end of the land and now I was balanced on a fine line between two worlds, the known and the unknown, the familiar and the unfamiliar. When it was time to leave, there was no question in my mind as to which way I would turn.

I felt humbled by the sea, distressed about the land and what is happening to it.

Ages ago, it is said, a creature emerged from the sea and learned to live and breathe and eventually to walk on the land.

There is no return.

To come to Alma and to walk as far as you can toward the sea is to know this.

Outdoor Music

We had been out after lake trout and now Arden Robertson and I were sitting side-by-side in the stern of a charter boat coming off Lake Michigan.

Arden, a retired Sturgeon Bay post office employee, was telling a story about rabbit hunting. He was describing the excitement, the baying of the hounds and the time, near a road, when a driver stopped and shouted at him: "What's the matter, are you blind? Two rabbits just crossed right in front of you. Why didn't you shoot?"

And Arden had answered: "Because when I shoot, the music stops."

It struck me again that there is a kind of a music that accompanies every outdoor activity and every outdoorsman worth his salt hears it.

I hear it often.

It's in the whistle of a flyline, looped high overhead and just beginning the forward thrust that will send it streaking toward its target.

It's in the singing of a reel when a big fish strikes and heads for open water.

It's in the squeak of an oarlock and in the barely audible swish of a canoe paddle.

You can hear it on a woodland trail, in the rustle of leaves under a booted foot. And you can hear it in the water rushing past a pair of waders in the middle of a stream.

There is bird music, the sound of a duck gliding over a blind on set wings, the gabbling sound of a skein of geese winding high over a marsh, the sweet serenades of the song birds and the raucous calls of the crows and the jays.

There is music in the sound of rain on a tent and in the clatter of acorns falling on a cabin roof.

There is music in the sound of horses' hooves searching for footing on a rocky mountain trail.

And there is music in the waves breaking rhythmically on a lonely stretch of Lake Michigan beach.

You can hear music in the morning sounds, in the jangling of an alarm clock sometime just before dawn, in the clatter of the grates when the ashes are being shaken down in the wood stove, in the squealing of a pump handle and, before long, in the bubbling of a coffee pot and the sizzling of bacon in the pan.

At night, the music is more subtle, but you still can hear it — if you listen.

It might be in the quiet conversation and soft laughter of a group of men huddled around a campfire.

And there is the nightsong of the campfire, itself; the constant sharp snapping of a burning cedar log or the occasional explosive pop from a chunk of white oak.

There is night music in the soft hiss of a gas lantern, in the breeze stirring up the aspen leaves; there even is a certain kind of music in the desperate whine of a bloodthirsty mosquito.

There's another kind of outdoor music that's perhaps the most stirring of all.

This song starts with the snort of a buck on a frosty November morning; or in the October woods when a ruffed grouse thunders out from under your feet; or on a lake in June, when the force of a strike tells you that you're into a big one.

Now the music is loud and clear. It comes from the fierce pounding of your own heart — and that, my friend, is the sweetest song you'll ever hear.

We Are Seekers of Quiet Places

Having spent a good part of my life in search of quiet places, I have come to the conclusion that there is a difference between quiet and silence.

Silence is the absence of sound; quiet is the absence of irritating sound.

Depending on the level of tolerance for noise, what constitutes a quiet place for one person may be bedlam for another.

All of us have been in homes where there are children running and shouting and screaming and crying all at the same time. In some cases, the mother is on the verge of hysteria; in others, she is the picture of serenity.

The second mother has tuned herself out. She has created her own quiet place in her mind. I think we can all do this to some degree.

We can't run off to a mountain top or a trout stream every time the noise of modern society closes in on us, so we learn to cope.

We learn to sort out the sounds, to develop our own level of tolerance, to determine which are pleasant and familiar and which are irritating and nerve-jangling.

Often, they are the same sounds.

I was raised near a railroad track and the steam engines chugged and whistled by during the night. It was a pleasant and soothing sound. But if a steam engine chugged up to my front door now and let out a blast of its whistle, I would jump out of my skin.

Later, I spent a couple of years on an Air Force flight line and slept next to a building where jet engines were tested all night long. I would wake up only when the noise stopped and I would wonder what was wrong.

Imagine a hotel room high above the city and from an open window you hear the muffled sounds from the streets below. Not at all unpleasant.

Now take the elevator down and step out onto the sidewalk. The honking of horns and the squeeling of brakes is enough to set your teeth on edge. Same sounds. Different perspective.

The most irritating noises of all are the sounds that startle and threaten. We can eliminate most of these simply by stepping inside and closing a door.

I believe we have a greater tolerance for noise than we realize. Man, by nature, is a gregarious creature. He is a joiner. He likes the sights and sounds of other people. He likes civilization. He says he likes to be alone, but he really doesn't, not too often or for too long at a time.

Man generally is frightened by the wilderness and with a few exceptions has little urge to return to it.

He will return to the fringes of it, to the campgrounds and the hotels and the resorts and the guided nature tour, but he seldom will penetrate it alone. What he fears most is the silence — and his own thoughts.

When a city man wants to get away from it all, he takes his civilization with him. He loads a mountain of gear in and on top of his car and heads up a busy highway to spend a weekend on a noisy, crowded lake.

The trapper and the lumberjack suffer from cabin fever and they run into town to whoop it up on a Saturday night.

Only a man with a hangover really appreciates absolute silence ("Get me an aspirin out of that box, please, and don't slam the lid.").

For every man alone in the wilderness, there are thousands cheering in crowded stadiums and gymnasiums and flocking to race tracks and rock concerts or sitting in front of blaring TV sets.

We have come a long way from early man who huddled in the entrance of his cave listening for dinosaur footsteps.

But there still are those among us who seek an occasional respite from noise.

We are the seekers of the quiet places.

We find these places along the trout streams and on the quiet canoeing waters; we find them in the marshes and the meadows and the woods. We are soothed by the babbling of a brook or by the sound of the wind in the pines. Sometimes these places are far from civilization, more often they are not.

There are other quiet places, too, a house at night, when everyone else is asleep and there is only the soft crackling of an oak log burning in the stove, the quiet table in the corner of a crowded restaurant, the hushed whispering and rustling of pages in the reading room of a public library.

Quiet, sometimes, is only something that goes on in the mind.

The Quiet People Are Making Some Noise

Let's say just for the sake of discussion that you can divide everyone who enjoys the outdoors into two distinct groups — the quiet people and the noisy people.

You can't, of course, because nobody fits that neatly into a mold. But a pattern seems to have been developing through the years.

The quiet people would be the hikers, bikers, snowshoers, wilderness campers, nature photographers, bird-watchers, cross-country skiers, and canoeists.

The noisy people are the snowmobilers, trail bike riders, power boaters, and, sometimes, hunters.

It isn't easy to be a quiet man. Sometimes it seems like the world is full of bullies and every time you turn around one of them is kicking sand in your face.

Example: There is a marsh that abounds with wildlife and wildflowers. You like to go there occasionally and explore. One day you go and it's filled with earth-moving equipment. It's being drained and filled in for an apartment complex. "We're running out of room," the developer says.

Example: There is a beautiful river, a quiet river for canoeing. The Corps of Engineers builds a dam, and soon there is a lake for power boaters and water skiers.

The quiet people continue to lose ground. Mountain trails become divided highways. More people want to see the view from the top. Dams are built on the Colorado River and tourists can visit the canyons by boat.

Conservationist David Brower says, "We don't flood the Sistine Chapel so tourists can get nearer the ceiling." Nobody pays any attention.

The noisy people have power and influence on their side. They spend money on machines and gasoline and oil. They buy guns and ammunition. The companies that produce these things grow and, to protect themselves, they hire lawyers and lobbyists. Their influence expands.

That's progress. And how can you fight progress? Snowshoes and canoes don't burn gasoline. Cameras do not kill. They can't support big corporations. The little old man in Maine who makes snowshoes can't afford a lobbyist, and he probably won't be around long anyway. There already are plastic snowshoes on the market.

Every once in a while, the quiet man get a concession from the government. He doesn't get lakes and super highways. He gets things like the abandoned railroad beds. They dump a little gravel on them and say, "Here's a place for your hiking and bicycling."

Even there, there are strings attached. The railroad bed runs through a public hunting area. The Department of Natural Resources says, "Well, we'll have to do something about that some day."

There is a maximum use policy for outdoor areas. Snowmobilers use the trails in the winter. The winter hiker fears for his life. Same answer.

Noisy people are, by nature, a gregarious lot. They travel in herds, they organize clubs. In unity lies strength. The majority rules.

The quiet man always has been a loner. That's his nature. He questioned but never complained too loudly.

If he joined anything it was something like the Sierra Club, which was largely an outing organization for old gaffers and little old ladies. Nobody took it seriously. Until now.

Has the quiet man been pushed too far? What's happened? The Sierra Club has turned into a militant conservation organization. It has been fighting for wilderness areas. It has stopped a number of dam building projects. Maybe it isn't too late.

The quiet man is fighting back. Friends of the Earth and other organizations have sprung up to join the battle.

At first they were only pests, but their numbers grew, and their leaders gained in expertise.

The courts started to listen. The government started to listen.

The term "environmental impact statement" was heard in the land.

A coalition of environmental organizations is making its voice heard in the nuclear power issue.

Motors have been banned on Devils Lake and a few other small Wisconsin lakes. The splash of the paddle and the creak of the oarlock is heard once more.

The highway builders are listening and the lumber companies and the automobile manufacturers and even the dam builders.

The quiet man is starting to make a little noise.

The little old lady in tennis shoes is taking on the hairy-chested he-man in hobnail boots — and winning.

It is written that "the meek shall inherit the Earth."

Sometimes it gets just too hard to wait.

Arne's Alaska

There is a community in Alaska called Anchor Point.

It's on the Kenai Peninsula where the Anchor River spills into Cook Inlet, roughly 200 miles south of Anchorage and 25 miles north of Homer.

There are moose there, and bear and, during the spring and fall runs, the river is a major route of the king salmon and the steelhead.

It was to Anchor Point that Arne brought his bride shortly after World War II.

Arne Murto was a Minnesota Finn, young, blond, wiry, self-sufficient, independent. He attacked everything he did with a kind of joyful abandon.

He came to Alaska, he said, "to get out of the rat race."

So he homesteaded his 160 acres at Anchor Point and set about putting his personal kingdom in order.

The first building was a one-room spruce-log cabin on the south bank of the river, not far from the only other building at the Point, a combination post office and general store.

Then he built the Anchor Inn, a two-room log building with a few tables and a bar. Here he offered lunches and beer to the few travelers and hunters and fishermen who strayed his way.

It wasn't long before the family began to outgrow the cabin by the river, so he picked another location out on the point facing the inlet. And he built a bigger log house, the one that was his home during the two years that I knew him.

He turned the old log cabin over to me whenever I went down there to hunt or fish. He wouldn't charge for it. If you stayed at Anchor Point and patronized Arne's Inn, you were his guest.

He didn't really even like to charge for the food and beer he served. But his wife, Thelma, was of a more practical nature and had learned to keep a watchful eye on him.

Arne, when I knew him, was a truly contented man. The Pacific Ocean was his front yard. He could stand in front of his home and watch the waves wash onto the beach. He could dig razor clams there at dead-low tide. He could watch the gulls overhead and, at certain times of the year, he could watch hair seals frolicking playfully in the shallows just offshore.

His back yard was miles and miles of Alaskan wilderness, of unfenced muskeg, forest and clear-running streams.

Arne learned all the tricks of living off the land.

He became a master of the double-bitted axe and he could fell, trim and notch a spruce log while you still were standing there thinking about it.

He discovered he could burn the coal that broke off coal reefs in the inlet and floated in with the tide. Winter fuel was there for the taking whenever the tide went out.

He built a saw rig behind the inn where he sawed lumber for his own use and often for other homesteaders.

He set up a cantankerous portable generator to provide electricity at the inn. It took a lot of tinkering to keep it going. Sometimes keeping the lights on became almost a full-time job.

And, although Arne wanted no part of the rat race, he was not anti-social. He was one of the friendliest men I've met. He loved company. He was in his element presiding over his bar or guiding hunters and fishermen through the Kenai Peninsula bush.

Sometimes I think he loved, most of all, to dance. And, as a polka dancer, I've seen no equal. He was Fred Astaire in a wool shirt and rubber boots, gliding gracefully over a rough-hewn cabin floor.

I lost track of Arne when I left Alaska some 20 years ago. It was just one of those things. We never kept in touch.

But I thought of him again not long ago when I was reading an article about the Kenai Peninsula in the Alaska magazine.

"People-wise and industry-wise," the article said, "this is really where the action is . . . oil wells . . . refineries . . . gas wells . . . homesteading giving way to oil wells and dollars and related metropolitan progress. Kenai, Soldotna and other Kenai Peninsula cities are booming."

I wonder if Arne stayed or if he moved on. I wonder how he felt when he saw the rat race closing in on him again.

Some Men Wrestle with Guilt

You probably have noticed that there are among us those who are able to accomplish life's necessary little tasks and still seem to have plenty of time for fishing and other outdoor activities.

While accomplishing all of this, you also may have noticed they seem to be conspicuously relaxed and unhurried.

These are the men who, by opening day, have their gardens in, their bushes pruned, their lawns raked, their houses painted and trimmed. They also have a supply of dry flies, hand-tied and perfect, the kind that don't unravel when they hit the water. Their waders never leak.

I long have admired such men. I have studied them and questioned them. I have yet to understand exactly what it is that makes them so.

The best I can come up with is that they seem to have been blessed with an ability for organization that cannot be learned or copied; that it is a kind of gift, a natural ability akin to being able to play the piano or produce great art or speak several foreign languages fluently.

The thing I envy most about them is that they are able to fish without guilt.

Let's face it. Most of us, when we are fishing, are nagged by the realization that we really should be doing something else, something much more important.

Our house is covered with aluminum siding and is relatively maintenance free, but there have been times through the years when the trim was badly in need of paint. Last year was one of those times. I started the job in the early spring and finished it just before the first snowfall, all but the garage door and the basketball bounding board which I will try to finish this year.

The point is that all the while I was fishing, there was a small voice inside me telling me I should be home painting.

This year I vowed to get all of my spring work done before I go fishing.

It is not going well. The weather has not been exactly cooperative, but I can't blame it all on the weather because, when it comes to organization, I am my own worst enemy.

I don't know if it's something I have inherited or something that was drilled into me in my youth, but I believe that work comes before play, that play is a reward that must be earned. I believe it, but I don't necessarly agree with it.

It begins, I suppose, when your mother says: "Make your bed and pick up your room before you go out and play."

It is encouraged early in school when you discover that it takes several hours of classroom work to earn a short recess.

It is enforced by the drill sergeant who drives you to the point of breaking before he relaxes and says, "All right, smoke if you got 'em."

It is reinforced, later in life, when you accept the fact that you must work 50 weeks of the year in order to get two weeks off.

And that is why I am spending these early spring mornings foraging for firewood when, were I composed of weaker moral fiber, I could be fishing for trout.

There is another kind of man and I am reminded of one in particular. He lives in a nice house among a lot of other nice houses in a nice part of town. His house is conspicuous because it is the one that needs painting; it is the one with the weeds growing through the cracks in the driveway, the one with the broken window pane in the garage door.

He fishes, too, but he is not concerned about the condition of his property. He likes it that way. He views it as a necessary product of his lifestyle, the result of a special kind of careful neglect. It is, he maintains, part of his image. He is not nagged by feelings of guilt.

He often fishes with the first type of man and the two are compatible.

They share, I have noticed, one common trait: They do not waste their time worrying about stupid things.

I know and fish with both kinds of men and, although I am not exactly either kind, I enjoy their company. Why they put up with me, I don't know. Perhaps I serve as a reminder of what they might have been had they been born less fortunate.

A Chance Meeting

Ever notice what happens when two strange dogs meet, how they walk around each other kind of stiff-legged and bristling?

There is a lot of sniffing and growling and it's touch and go for awhile. Then it either ends in a fight or they run off together, barking playfully and wagging their tails.

I was reminded of this one day earlier this summer when another fisherman and I met, purely by chance, on a stretch of sand country trout stream that turned out to be both his favorite and mine.

I was there first. It was mid-afternoon and I had just driven down the sand lane to the stream and parked, hidden from view from the lane, in a grove of scrub oak.

I was standing by the tailgate putting on my waders when another car drove in. I watched the driver out of the corner of my eye. His jaw dropped a couple of notches when he saw me.

I nodded. He nodded back, carefully. "You coming or going?" he asked. I told him I was just starting. His jaw dropped another notch.

He parked a polite distance away and got out and began puttering with his equipment.

He watched while I threaded the line through the guide of my flyrod. I began to feel sorry for him. I was there first. I had squatter's rights. He was the intruder and he knew it.

But he seemed a pleasant fellow and it could have been the other way around. Just a couple of minutes would have made the difference.

"Look," I said, "I don't need the whole stream. There's plenty of room here for both of us. We'll split it up."

His eyes brightened. "What part do you want?" he asked.

"Well," I answered, "I usually like to head downstream about a quarter of a mile to that fringe of woods and work my way back up to here again."

"Fine," he said. "I'll take the upper part."

"If you'd rather go downstream, I don't really care," I offered.

"No," he said. "I'm only going to fish with worms this afternoon anyway. I'll switch to flies later on, maybe this evening if there's a hatch."

I knotted a fly on the end of my leader and gave it a yank. The leader snapped. "Damn!" I said.

"What's the matter?" he asked.

"My leader broke," I said, "and it's my last one."

He had me there. He could have sent me all the way back to town for more. But he didn't

"Here," he said, "take a couple of mine."

"I'll buy them from you," I offered.

"No," he said. "I won't take any money for them."

We split up then and I didn't see him again for the rest of the afternoon.

It was a beautiful sunny afternoon. I worked my way slowly upstream. I caught three or four small trout and released them. I sat in the grass and watched the sky. I climbed a tree, waders and all, to retrieve a royal coachman, hung in its upper reaches by a careless backcast.

It was almost evening when I saw him again, standing on a grassy point at a bend in the stream. He was carrying a wicker creel and he opened the lid to show me his catch. There were three good-sized browns.

"Nice catch," I said.

"Thanks," he answered.

We sat on the bank and talked awhile. He was from Oshkosh and had driven to the stream for the same reason I had, not so much to fish, just to be in a place he liked. We discovered we had a friend in common in Madison.

"There's a deep hole with a log in the bottom of it under that tangle of brush in the next bend up there," he offered. "I saw a big trout rise there earlier. He won't take a worm, but maybe he'll take a fly."

I waded to the bend while he watched and flicked a fly under the brush and around the bend with a kind of awkward sidearm cast.

There was a swirl and a sharp tug, but I had too much slack in my line. It was a big trout and he shook off before I could set the hook. I couldn't raise him again.

"I guess I'll have to leave him for you," I told my friend.

Night was coming on and there almost certainly would be a hatch. I wanted to stay, but I was due back in Madison.

"Looks like you're going to have the best fishing all to yourself," I said. "I have to leave."

"That's too bad," he answered. "I wish you could stay.'

We shook hands and, as I walked away, he already had abandoned his worms and was tying on a big yellow fly.

I stopped on the high bank on the other side of the stream and looked down at him once more. He had entered the water and was playing out line for a cast.

It could have been my imagination or maybe just a trick played by the late evening light, but I'll swear he was wagging his tail.

Who's in a Hurry to Be an Oldtimer?

A friend of mine is fond of saying about me: "Hopkins is the only man I know who can hardly wait to be old."

I suspect there is some truth in what he says. I long have been an observer and admirer of what generally is referred to in the vernacular of the outdoorsman as "the oldtimer."

You know them when you see them. They are the old men with the battered felt hats and the faded wool shirts and the baggy pants and the well-greased boots, the men with gray hair and eyes that are perpetually youthful.

They are largely the products of misspent lives — lives dedicated to the pursuit of trout and muskies and grouse and ducks and deer.

They know where the trout pools are and the grouse coverts. They can track a deer and call a duck. They can sharpen a knife until they can shave with it and use a double-bitted axe like a surgeon's scalpel. They can build a campfire in the rain and fire up a contrary backwoods cabin woodstove and make it sing.

Through it all they smile and laugh through features that have been carved by the summer sun and the winter wind.

They are quiet men, by and large, but, when the occasion calls for it, they will sit up half the night telling the old stories, keeping alive the memories of the woods and the fields and the marshes and the streams.

The stories? You've probably heard them or their variations.

There is "Old Mossback," the giant trout who lives in a deep pool under a tangle of roots and has successfully outwitted even the best of fishermen for years. Sometimes "Old Mossback" is a musky or a largemouth bass. It doesn't seem to matter.

There is the story about the time Fred fell into the Wolf River and emerged a few hundred yards downstream with a limit of rainbows trapped in his waders.

There is the best-damned-bird-dog-I-ever-had story, the day the camp cook got mad and quit story, the breaking through the ice when it was 30 below zero story, and the "dead" buck that got up and ran away story.

There is the gun that wouldn't fire story, the broken snowshoe story, and the worst backlash I ever saw story.

There is the lost in the woods story and, along with it, the story about the time old Charley took the little woman deer hunting, put her on a stand before dawn and forgot all about her until sometime after supper.

She still was sitting on the stump when he found her. She stood up, pointed to a nine-point buck in the shadows a few yards away and said: "I shot it, now you can drag it out."

A younger man, privileged to be in the company of the oldtimers, soon learns to keep his place, a kind of combination of apprentice and servant.

He is the one who pushes the boat away from the shore and gets his foot wet trying to jump in at the last minute.

He unloads the car, cleans the fish, carries the wood and runs the errands.

He helps the cook and he sets the table and pours the coffee. He does the dishes and sweeps out the cabin.

He loses at cards and he is the cheerful butt of many jokes.

In turn, he is patiently instructed in the lore of the outdoors.

He learns how to tie flies, gaff a musky, place a set of decoys, handle a shotgun, field-dress a deer, pole a canoe, set a downrigger, read a stream and filet a salmon.

He learns respect for the outdoors and for the men and the creatures that inhabit it.

He is in no hurry. There is no quick way out of his apprenticeship. The only requirements for graduation are age and experience. His time will come.

One magic night there will be an empty chair in front of the fire and he will sink gratefully into it, tired and weary from a day afield.

There will be a younger man around to do the dishes and sweep out the cabin.

The transition will have begun.

I am not an oldtimer yet and, in spite of what my friend says, I can wait.

Being an oldtimer carries a tremendous amount of responsibility. I am not ready. I have a few years to go and a lot to learn.

When my time comes, I hope I can measure up.

Bud Laugen, left, and Hopkins with a Flambeau Flowage musky.

Chapter Six

BUMMING AROUND

Bud Laugen

I first ran into Bud Laugen when I went with a bunch of guys on a Lake Michigan fishing trip out of Sturgeon Bay. That was 10 or 12 years ago. I didn't quite know what to think of him then, and I don't quite know what to think of him now.

Through the years we have shared a few trout streams, a few sunsets on northern musky lakes, a drink or two with good friends during the long evenings in northwoods cabins.

He is 73 or 74 years old. He outfishes me. He beats me at pool. He beats me at euchre. I played a round of golf with him once and he beat me then, too. I didn't mind being bested at golf by an old man, but I did mind losing to someone who used a putter for fairway shots, and who jumped up and down and cackled when he got closer to the pin than I did.

There are those who claim Laugen is just lucky. There are those who, secretly at least, are convinced he cheats. I happen to believe it's neither. It's just that Laugen, you see, is smarter than he looks. A lot of people are taken in by that, but not me. Not anymore.

Oh, I know there was the night he got me lost in a swamp up on the Mecan River. He claims he didn't do it on purpose, but I know better.

And there was the time he almost convinced me I would catch more fish if I learned to cast left-handed. It almost worked, but I got wise when I glanced around after two or three casts and caught him trying to stifle a grin.

In other years and other times he might have been a peddler of hair restorer or youth elixer, a con man always only one step ahead of discovery.

He has this foolish little mustache and he plays this country boy role that suggests he might be an easy mark. The only giveaway, once you get to know him, is the gleam in his eyes.

The gleam should tell you he is not the rube he would have you believe. This man came out of a backwoods Minnesota farm and worked his way through the University of Wisconsin at a time when every farm boy didn't go on to school. This is a gullible country boy who subscribes to scientific journals and hides them under Sports Afield magazines on his coffee table.

Among things he enjoys most is a good joke on himself. At breakfast the other morning he told me about the first deer he killed, years ago, with an arrow.

In those days, deer killed by bow hunters had to be checked by a warden to make sure there were no gunshot wounds. Laugen was in a hurry to get to work so his hunting companion said he would drop it off at a butcher shop and have the warden come in and check it later.

Apparently it was a pretty small deer and when the warden came into the butcher shop the next day he asked where he could find it. "It's right over there," the butcher supposedly replied. "You can't see it from here. It's behind that ring of bologna."

Knowing all this about Laugen, I continue to fish with him and enjoy his company. It could be, I suppose, only because I am convinced that someday I might get the best of him at something, anything.

But I know there is more to it than that. A few years ago, for instance, when I caught my first musky up on the Flambeau Flowage, Laugen was the one who understood, who still listened to my story long after the others had abandoned me.

I like his company, too, because I know I continue to learn from him, even in defeat. And, probably most of all, I like his company because he makes the most of little pleasures and, certainly, because he is younger at heart than most young men I know.

Indian Summer Canoeing

It's funny how you remember some days, how they start and how they end and all the things in between.

Sometimes it has something to do with the weather, or where you were, or what you were doing — and sometimes it's a combination of all of these.

Sometimes it's just a little thing that starts a day right and makes it different from the others. It might be the sight of a hawk circling lazily above a patch of mist rising over a river bottom pothole or it might be the reflection of the morning Sun captured for just a moment on the dewy bright-orange surface of a bittersweet berry, deep in the woods where the Sun doesn't often reach.

There is an Indian Summer day, late in October, that starts like this, at a canoe-landing on a river you know well, that you are looking forward to running once more before the winter comes.

So there is meaning in this day because it might be the last trip for a long time.

You slide the canoe from the truck onto your shoulders and carry it to the river. You feel its weight through the pads on the yoke, and it feels good. A canoe is meant to be carried this way. It never was designed to be dragged awkwardly through the brush and sand like a giant dead beast.

You roll it over and set it in the river where it rests quietly, the bow pulled up on shore, the stern rolling gently in the current that is sweeping under it.

The water is cold now in the late fall and you are wearing chest waders because you know there will be times you'll have to get out to drag the canoe over a shallow gravel bar or through a deadfall. You wear a heavy wool sweater, but only because it is still early morning. You know you soon will be paddling in your shirtsleeves.

You load a pack and a Thermos into the canoe; then you climb into the stern, push off from the bank, and, with a sweep of the paddle, swing the bow around and point it downstream. You feel it when the current picks you up, and, with another dip of the paddle, you are part of the river.

For the next few hours you will go where the river takes you. You will be in a quiet world that winds through steep hills, past well-manicured farm fields and through dense tangles of woods. There will be huge rock outcroppings, mossy valleys, hemlock groves and marsh.

The sounds you hear will be the murmur of the river, the cries of hawks and crows, and the chattering of the dark clouds of blackbirds gathering in the treetops along the banks.

The leaves are fallen now, and the skeletons of the trees stand naked against the autumn sky.

You remember how it looked in the spring when the world was new and the river bottom was lush and green and sprinkled with colorful wildflowers.

You remember the full, ripe growth of summer, and you remember the heat and how you canoed the river in shorts and tennis shoes.

You remember stopping to look at the river in the winter, when it is locked in ice with only a little open water where it runs fast over the riffles and around the bends.

You do not hurry on this day because you want it to last. You want it to be a memory for the long winter months ahead.

When a great blue heron slowly takes to the sky from around the bend ahead of you, you nose the bow into the bank and stop and watch it go. You study its awkward flight, the great flapping wings, the long legs dragging behind, and you wonder how such a bird can fly. You watch it until it disappears into a treetop perch along the river far downstream.

When you have been on the river a long time and you are hungry you pull onto a gravel bar and you get out and unload the pack. There is bread in it, and apples, and a Thermos of coffee. In another Thermos there are big slices of hot ham. You sit on the point of gravel under the October Sun and while you eat you watch the river and the hills around it.

At the end of the trip, when you are loading the canoe back on the truck, the Sun already is disappearing and only a red tip of it is still visible above the horizon.

There is a chill in the air again, and soon the evening mist will begin rising from the river.

You drive home and there is an open fire waiting. You stand before it and warm yourself, and you think about the day. It has been a good day.

An Old Dog and a Young Pup

Autumn makes its entrance slowly. It is most noticeable now, in the beginning, in the lowlands, in the creek bottoms and the marshes.

It is most noticeable, too, in the early morning, in the chill that is in the air before the sun burns it away, in the cold dew on the marsh grasses, in the chattering of the birds flocking for their annual flight to the south and warmer climates, in the sight of an open milkweed pod hanging limply from its stem.

There is a subtle change in the breeze. Its touch is a little more persistent, in early autumn, and it seems to whisper: "Walk with me, my friend; we will explore this new season together."

I felt it in the air, through the bedroom window, when I woke up this morning.

The dogs, I think, felt it, too, and they were there at my feet while I dressed. They watched me, waiting for a sign. They can tell by the clothes I choose if they are going to be included in my plans for the day.

I hadn't planned to take them. This was to be a quiet morning, perhaps my last morning of this year on a small trout stream. I would travel light, with only a flyrod and a small box of grasshopper flies. No net. No waders. No bulky fishing vest.

I would sit alone, on a streambank, soaking up the warmth of the sun. I would watch the water carefully for the telltale spreading ring, a sign that a trout was rising to pluck a grasshopper or perhaps some other insect from the surface.

The dogs licked at my boots, tails wagging, when I bent to pull them on. They whined eagerly when I took an old woolen cardigan sweater from a closet hanger.

I reached down to pat the old dog. Her eyes pleaded with me to take her along. It had been a long time since we roamed the woods together.

I picked the dog whistle from the top of the dresser and hung it, from its leather thong, around my neck. The dogs bounded for the front door.

We drove through the Dane County countryside, Highway PD where it runs through a marsh and across the upper reaches of the Sugar River. We turned on J and then G and then, finally, Highway 92 where it runs through the village of Mount Vernon.

The dogs were restless. They rode with their noses stuck out of the truck windows, sniffing the air in anticipation. Penny, the old dog, knew we were near our destination. She had been there before. This was the first time for Stella (I didn't name her; my daughters did), but she seemed to sense and reflect the older dog's eagerness.

I pulled off the road and parked on a public fishing-grounds access path.

"I will let them run for awhile," I thought, "then I will move downstream and leave them in the truck while I fish."

We walked up the path, which had grown over during the summer. My boots soon were covered with mud.

Penny is about 10 years old now and showing her age. She is graying around the eyes and muzzle, and she has lost the spring in her step. She is content to walk slowly and carefully consider her surroundings. We are a lot alike, in a way, and I think she senses that, too.

Stella is a pup, about six or seven months, and clearly was impatient with us old folks. With the boundless energy of youth, she ranged far ahead. Penny stayed closer to my side, making only occasional skirmishes into the brush along the path.

I called them to the truck and drove another mile or so downstream, stopping this time at the head of a graveled lane that leads, eventually, to the creek.

I opened the back, removed my flyrod and closed it again. The dogs looked at me reproachfully through the window. I opened the door and let them out.

Puppies chase butterflies. Stella discovered one as we approached the creek and pursued it to the streambank, where she made one final desperate lunge and ended up in the water. Check off one trout pool.

Both dogs found something of interest in the nearby tall grass, and I tried to slip quietly away. Maybe they wouldn't find me for awhile.

I chose another deep pool at a bend in the stream, tied a grasshopper fly on the end of my leader and began letting out line for a cast. Stella must have spotted the motion in the air, because by the time the fly hit the water she was standing at the edge of the stream barking at it. I gave up. It was late morning, and I was due at work soon anyway.

I sat for a time in the shade of an old willow and watched them romp. Then I called them to me, and once again we headed for the truck.

A mile or so down the road, I turned to look in the back seat. Both were sound asleep.

Stella, I imagined, was dreaming foolish puppy dreams of grasshoppers and butterflies.

Penny's dreams I think would be of other autumns, of other times and other places, of misty mornings in the creek bottoms, of the sound and smell of a ruffed grouse thundering out of a woodland thicket, of sunny autumn days with fallen leaves crackling underfoot, of crisp autumn evenings by an open fire.

She would dream of these things, I think, because I do at this time of the year. And we are, after all, a lot alike.

Some Good Wisconsin Country

There is some good country up in south-central Wisconsin. It's an almost flat country, gently rolling at the most, and at first glance it looks scrubby and barren and useless, but it is not.

Men live on the edges of it and in little pockets of woods here and there; but in between the farms and the hunting and fishing cabins are acres and acres of woods and marshes and miles of clear sand-bottom trout streams.

It is a land that belongs mostly to the wild things that inhabit it.

A man will see a few deer browsing in the clearings along the roadsides in the evening and know that there are many more, deep in the woods.

He will wade a stream and catch a few small trout and know that they are the easy ones; that there are huge, wary browns lying in the deep holes and under tangles of roots that he will not catch unless he is very good or very lucky.

A man can spend a day fishing in this country, and then, for all the days until he comes up here again, he will remember what it was like.

He will remember driving down a narrow town road and seeing the deer, and then turning off and driving down a sand road into the woods, and, after that, the stillness and quiet when he stopped and got out of the car and walked to the stream.

That's the way it starts when he thinks about it, and soon it all comes back in his mind.

There is a small trail that crosses a meadow and he follows it to a fringe of brush that borders the stream where it enters the woods at the meadow's edge.

The trail through the patch of brush is narrow, and he has to stoop to get through the tangle of limbs and branches. He carries his flyrod low and points it ahead of him, guiding it carefully through. The trail at his feet is soft and muddy now. He can feel it and smell it, and, when he looks down, he sees that there are deer tracks in it.

Then, there is the stream. It is clear and fast and about knee-deep. The bottom is firm, and he does not sink in. It will be easy wading.

He stands quietly, at the beginning, giving himself time to become accustomed to the feel of the water. He hears a bobwhite quail and he looks around but does not see it.

There is a small pool behind a sunken log a few feet upstream, and he begins stripping line from the reel and looping it loosely in his left hand.

He begins to false cast, feeding the line out through the guides. When he has the distance, he shoots the line forward and lets it drop on the water.

The leader rolls over, and the fly drops softly to the surface. There is a splash and a flash of silver, and the trout is gone.

The man moves on upstream. Perhaps it is not good anyway to catch a trout on the first cast, he thinks to himself. It would be disappointing if there were no more.

He wades slowly. He does not want to hurry. He misses another one but stands and waits awhile, then casts again at the same spot.

This time he is ready, and he feels it when he sets the hook, the solid feeling that tells him the trout is still there. He holds the rod tip high and strips in the line. The trout is a small one and is soon in the net.

The man steps out of the stream, feeling pleased with himself, and sits down on the grassy bank and lights his pipe.

The water drips from his waders, and there is some sand stuck to them, and there is the smell of fish on his hands. He is part of this stream and this meadow now, and he feels good about that, too.

He works his way upstream this way, all through the afternoon, and takes three more trout in the same way.

And when it is time to go, he leaves the stream and climbs a steep bank and walks back to the car, this time through a small patch of scrub oak woods.

That's how he remembers this day when he thinks about it. And he will think about it often — and for a long time.

October Only Comes Once a Year

There are some days that, more than others, seem to have been designed with quiet walking in mind.

They are days that are sunny and bright and neither too warm nor too cold but just crisp enough to be physically invigorating and spiritually stimulating.

It helps if there are a few fallen leaves to crackle underfoot.

It is frustrating when these days happen to fall during the week and if one is forced to view them through an office window.

There was one particular day like that not too long ago, a day on which I was torn between going into the office and playing hooky and heading for the woods.

"Would John Muir," I asked myself, "or Henry David Thoreau (I wonder if anyone ever called him Hank) have stayed inside on a day like this?"

The obvious answer: "Of course not."

I pulled on my baggy corduroy walking jacket and headed for the Arboretum.

The Arboretum is beautiful when the trees are in full color. It is inviting, but it is deceiving. It looks quiet and peaceful. It is not.

On this day, there was almost a steady string of cars, traveling in both directions and leaving clouds of exhaust fumes in their wakes. Motorcycle noise assaulted the ears. There were other people there — running, walking, biking, examining wildflowers and looking at birds.

I left and drove out of town to the country, to an area where there is a stream and some marshland, where there is meadow and woods, where there is humus instead of pavement, and area where there is true peace and quiet and even, if you will, serenity.

The leaves drop softly, and even the stream does not roar like big streams do; it gurgles quietly as it flows along its winding path through the bottomland.

Like Ferdinand the Bull, I am, by nature, a procrastinator. I tend to put things off until the last possible minute. I never do today that which could just as well be done tomorrow.

I am unproductive in an age when a man is judged by his productivity. I would rather loaf than mow a lawn or change a storm window or wash a car. I would rather fish than be a captain of industry.

And, in an age when hiking is popular, I prefer simply to walk, aimlessly, without time limits and without goals.

I find, as I approach 50, that I am in reasonably good health and physically capable of doing the things that are important to me. I can wade a trout stream, paddle a canoe, maneuver on skis, cut and split my own wood — and, in the evening in front of a fire, sit in a rocking chair and rock briskly while I read.

Why subject myself to body-building activities like jogging and long, strenuous hikes? I'll never run the Boston Marathon or quarterback the Green Bay Packers. I don't need the body of a 20-year-old. I've been 20.

I'd rather be 49; it's more fun.

So, with no pressure to hurry, I strolled for awhile along the edge of the stream. It was past the fishing season, but I stopped occasionally and stared into the clear pools in hopes of spotting a trout. I saw none.

Thinking about trout fishing is almost as good as doing it. A fisherman can stand at streamside, without rod and reel, and plot future strategy for fishing a particular riffle or pool.

If his imagination is good, he can float an imaginary fly along an undercut bank and into a tangle of willow roots. He can feel the strike; he can set the hook and play his imaginary trout perfectly before bringing it to net and carefully releasing it. It can be any size his conscience will allow.

When I had indulged my fantasy, I climbed a steep bank to a path that leads through a wide meadow. The dogs were with me. They would range far ahead, run back and jump up on me, then bound playfully away again.

A small patch of golden aspens beckoned from the distance, a sunlit island in a sea of grass. I found a comfortable spot there to rest, a comfortable tree trunk for my back.

I sat there for a time, contemplating the horizon, the tiny whisps of clouds high in an otherwise clear October sky, a distant hillside cloaked in brilliant shades of red and gold.

I dozed, briefly and was awakened by a wet tongue on my cheek.

I walked back across the meadow and down the bank to the stream, where I stopped long enough for the dogs to drink, than headed back to the car, slowly.

I suppose there were other things I should have done on that day, but October and Indian summer only come around once a year.

And they are like comfortable old friends to me now. It would be impolite to ignore them, wouldn't it?

Red-Winged Blackbirds

The retreating winter, in March, leaves a barren and desolate land in its wake.

The woods and the marshlands are drab and colorless. Last year's dead grasses cover the ground. Bushes and shrubs, crushed by the weight of the snow, lie twisted and bent.

A cold March wind whistles through bare tree limbs. A honeycombed coat of rotten ice covers the lakes and patches of snow remain on the hillsides and along the stream banks. Creeks, swollen with spring runoff, overflow and flood the lowlands.

The warming sun and the north wind are locked in an eternal tug-of-war. The outcome is predictable, only the length of the battle is uncertain.

It is to this scene that the hibernating animals awaken, it is to this land that the migrating birds return.

It is in this land, too, that another tug-of-war is about to begin anew — the war between the fishermen and the red-winged blackbirds.

The red-winged blackbirds are back. They were there, waiting to challenge me when I went to walk the edges of a marsh one day last week.

Probably no other creature is as fiercely protective of its territory.

A duck will try all kinds of fakery to lead you away from its nest. A turtle, sunning itself on an exposed log, will plop into the water and disappear at your approach. Startle a great blue heron and it will fly awkwardly away.

Disturb a squirrel and it will climb to a treetop and scold. A muskrat will graciously swim out of your way and let you pass. A feeding loon will keep its distance. A deer, upon getting your scent, will vanish, unseen. A snake will retreat before your footsteps.

A mother bear, unless you threaten her cubs, will gather them and run. A shadow cast across a stream will, as any fisherman knows, send a trout into hiding.

A red-winged blackbird will attack.

I once knew an old fisherman who, as far as I know, feared only two creatures: red-winged blackbirds and snakes.

There was one stream, a fine brook trout stream, he never would return to because a water snake once had dropped out of a tree there and landed at his feet.

I once asked him what he would do if a snake dropped down the front of his waders. "I think I would die right on the spot," was his answer. And he believed it.

This same man would panic when red-winged blackbirds began to intimidate him. He would flail at them with his rod and with his net and, finally, he would give in and abandon the stream.

He was a big man, well over six feet, and strong, and he endured, good-naturedly, more than his share of teasing because of his two aversions.

I have had my own encounters with red-winged blackbirds and there have been times, I will admit, when my own temptation to flee has been almost overpowering.

The most memorable encounter, and the one I came nearest to losing, was a few years ago on a northern Wisconsin flowage.

There is, near one end of the flowage, a floating bog that surrounds a deep pool. There are bass in the pool, 4- and 5- and 6-pound largemouths. I knew this, because I had caught them there before.

On this particular day I went there alone, in the late afternoon, in a canoe.

The outer edges of the bog are surrounded by water lilies. I fished the patches of open water between the lily pads while I worked the canoe closer and closer to a brush-choked channel leading to the center of the bog.

I was intent on the fishing and did not immediately notice that the numbers of red-winged blackbirds around me were increasing.

When I did notice, the hair on my wrists and the back of my neck stiffened, and if there had been any hair on my head I'm sure it would have stood up, too. There were goose pimples on my arms and I could feel the adrenalin coursing through my body.

It began with only a few, scolding from their perches on the tips of the marsh grasses. Soon, I was surrounded. Then they began closing in until there were great numbers of them cutting off my approach to the center of the bog, and they were intimidating me from perches only a few inches from my face.

I was tempted to back out of the channel. "Don't be ridiculous," I told myself, "they're only birds."

Using the paddle like a pole along the edge of the channel, I pushed the canoe to within casting distance of the pool and sat there, fishing, while the bolder of the birds made threatening swoops at my head and neck.

I had visions of my body washing up on shore some misty morning. A puzzled pathologist would fill out the autopsy report: "Pecked to death," it would read, "by a flock of red-winged blackbirds."

It was an eerie experience. There may have been a distant relative who billions of years ago took swamps and bogs for granted. I do not. I startle as easily as the heron and the deer.

I stayed there until I was satisfied that the bass, if there were any in the pool, were not going to bite; then I backed the canoe out of the channel and paddled to open water where I fished without interruption for the rest of the afternoon.

I realize there wasn't any real danger, and that I was just being foolish, but I still think of that incident whenever I am scolded from the edge of a stream by an angry red-winged blackbird.

I thought of it again the other day when I interrupted them while they were setting up spring housekeeping in a marsh.

Trees Make Sympathetic Listeners

I don't go to a psychiatrist. I suppose I have my own way of dealing with thoughts and ideas and problems that trouble me.

Often, when something is troubling me, I head for the woods or a quiet trout stream — a place where my mind is free to wander and I find that I come up with answers that are, at least, suitable to me.

One of my favorite "thinking places" isn't far out of the city. It's 15 or 20 minutes by car; then I walk about a quarter of a mile up a railroad track and another couple of hundred yards down a little-traveled town road.

There is a rusty old iron bridge there, with a small creek running under it. And, while the dog prowls the roadside weeds for scents of rabbits and field mice, I lean on the bridge and watch the water and bask in the Sun, if it's shining. Sometimes I go there in the rain.

I stood there one autumn day and watched a skein of geese pass overhead and listened to their honking. I have waded to the bridge, knee-deep in floodwater, in the early spring and felt the power of the changing season swirling around me.

It is quiet and pleasant now, in these late summer days, but there is a feeling of change in the air; a crisp tang in the breeze, for instance, that wasn't there a couple of weeks ago, a difference in the color of the marsh grass and weeds. The lowland probably already has been touched by frost.

There's an old willow near the bridge that's a good and sympathetic listener, and it knows how to keep a secret.

Don't get me wrong. I don't talk out loud to trees. But it does make a good silent companion, and sometimes it seems to know what I'm thinking and nods its great, green, shaggy head in agreement or disagreement.

It's not impossible. We know so little about our relationship with the natural world.

We are composed of the same elements that make up the Sun and the sky and the seas. We are of the same substance and structure as our fellow creatures.

Yet man is the only creature that is at war with his environment. I wonder if it is because, once we learned to reason, we had to establish our superiority over the other creatures and disassociate ourselves from the natural world in an attempt to deny our origins.

But there remains a fraternal relationship between man and other creatures that cannot be denied.

United States Supreme Court Justice William O. Douglas, in an autobiography called "Go East, Young Man," describes an incident at his Goose Prairie, Wash., home:

"As Prairie House was being built, I spent my time planting the meadow around the house and watering it. . . .

"One day as I sowed the seed I heard the baying of hounds on American Ridge to the north. Before long, I felt something touch my leg and, turning, I saw a doe deer standing close to me. Her eyes were dilated, she was breathing heavily, and she dripped with perspiration. Obviously she was near exhaustion and she had come to man for help. I had heard of such things before but never had believed them."

He describes how he led the way a half-mile to a river, with the doe following at his heels like a puppy. Then he slapped it on the rump and watched it swim to the other side and safety.

Is it possible that this will turn out to be one of man's major functions on Earth, to serve as a protector of the other creatures?

In geologic time, man hasn't been reasoning very long and perhaps we still are struggling and experimenting with it. Maybe our keeping of pets is only an early experiment, a test of the relationship between man and other animals. Or maybe we keep them around because we aren't quite sure of ourselves yet, aren't quite ready to stand completely alone.

Have you noticed that some of our entertainments and amusements are only pitiful copies of the awesome power displayed in nature?

The Northern Lights were visible over the city one night not long ago and I drove to the country and stood by the roadside and watched them, filled with wonder.

They are so seldom visible here that I was amazed that so few seemed to notice them. The streets and front yards should have been lined with people, all staring at the sky. But they weren't.

Still, every Fourth of July, people will drive for miles to sit in a crowded grandstand in a dusty fairground to swat mosquitoes and marvel at a few pathetic sparks called a fireworks display.

If a storm threatens, the display is cancelled and they all get up and go home.

What a show they would see if they remained there, in the grandstand, and listened to the thunder and felt the rain and watched the great bolts of lightning shoot across the summer skies.

I wonder if we aren't still in a very early, in a very primitive stage in the development of man, half reaching out to the unknown, half huddled in our caves, afraid of what we might find there.

I'd like to discuss this with my old willow tree by the old rusty bridge. But I'm afraid that, if it could answer, I know what it would say.

It would shake its great shaggy head and in a soft, deep kind of voice, it would whisper: "Hopkins, I think you should see a psychiatrist."

My Friend and Companion Thoreau

"There is a slumbering subterranean fire in nature," Henry David Thoreau wrote, "which never goes out, and which no cold can chill.

"It finally melts the great snow, and in January or July is only buried under a thicker or thinner cover. In the coldest days it flows somewhere, and the snow melts around every tree."

I think of this early one morning while I rest, leaning on a rusty Sugar River bridge rail and trying to warm my half-frozen fingers with whatever warm breath I can muster.

"Henry," I mutter through clenched and chattering teeth, "it appears that your fire has gone out."

My walk this morning is along a stretch of the Military Ridge Trail that runs along the river between Verona and Riley, in Dane County not far out of Madison. It is gray and cold. The thin cover of snow on the trail crunches under the tromping of my booted feet. There is no one else about. This little world of marsh and cattail and tiny, ice-fringed stream is mine alone to explore.

It would be a lonely walk, I suppose, if it were not for Henry, who frequently accompanies me on my morning outings. Sometimes there are others: John Muir, John Burroughs, Henry Beston, Loren Eiseley, even Augie Derleth — the natural philosophers who knew how to use their feet to free their minds.

But it is Henry — the pencilmaker, the surveyor, the flutist, the husbander of beans marching along joyously to the beat of his own drummer — who is my favorite companion.

At heart, he is a good sport and good company. His walks are frolics, adventures that unfold along the way, simple strolls rather than strenuous hikes.

Consider his famous "Fluvial Walk," during which he removed all of his clothing except his hat and spent a hot July day in 1852 wading the Assabet River in the altogether.

"I wonder," he mused, "if any Roman emperor ever indulged in such luxury as this, of walking up and down a river in torrid weather with only a hat to shade the head."

My winter stroll along the edge of the river could, I imagine, be a kind of "Frozen Fluvial Walk." Henry joins me somewhere along the way; he just kind of appears out of nowhere while I am leaning over the bridge railing, watching the river flow underneath.

He is wearing a woolen cap with the earflaps pulled down over his ears. His homespun coat is buttoned up over a woolen muffler that is wrapped around his skinny neck. His boots, one of three pair he keeps for walking, squeak as he walks up, even though they are well-greased with tallow.

He observes me watching the water and offers: "First of all a man must see, before he can say . . . At first blush a man is not capable of reporting truth; he must be drenched and saturated with it first." He does have a way with words, but sometimes he talks a little too much.

"C'mon, Henry," I answer, pushing away from the bridge, "walk on into Riley with me. There's a little watercress spring by the side of the trail just before you get into town that I want you to see."

He is adjusting his muffler. "The man who goes alone can start today," he says, a little testily I thought, "but he who travels with another must wait till that other is ready."

"But remember, Henry, it takes two to tango," I admonish, reminding him of the words of Pearl Bailey, another great philosopher. "Fix your damned muffler and let's get on with it."

He seems to be pouting a little. I think I hurt his feelings. "Hey, Henry," I say, giving him a friendly little jab in the ribs with my walking stick, "tell me something about the women in your life. How about that Mrs. Emerson? She must have been something, huh?"

Henry will have none of that. He ignores me and, instead, stoops to pick a plant from a patch of bare ground along the trail and carefully places it between the pages of an old music book he carries for pressing plants.

"It is remarkable," he informs me sternly, "how true each plant is to its season. Why should not (for example) the fringed gentian put forth early in the season, instead of holding on till the later part of September? I do not perceive enough difference in the temperature."

It might be just the weather, but this morning his condescending know-it-all attitude is beginning to get on my nerves.

"Who cares, Henry," I answer. "Sometimes I don't even know what you're talking about. Do you have to be so smug? Can't you ever talk like real people?"

"Tell me, my friend," he asks, "what have you ever written that will be remembered and quoted more than a century after after your death?"

"Well, let me see," I mutter uncertainly. "I once wrote: 'It matters not if the creel is empty, as long as the heart is full.' How about that?"

"That's not bad," Henry answers. "I'll give it a week or two, certainly not a hundred years."

"Well, then, how about this one," I retort, giving it my best shot:" 'No man ever lives long enough to use up all the paprika in his cupboard.' "

He is visibly startled. The smug smile on his face fades. Thoroughly beaten at his own game, he turns and vanishes into the thin morning air. I wave goodbye, although I am certain that I have not seen the last of him.

Sometimes, I think, it is not good for a man to spend too long alone in the cold.

Hopkins at the Colorado River in the bottom of the Grand Canyon.

Chapter Seven
SIFTING AND WINNOWING

Keeping a Low Profile

I got to work a little later than usual Thursday afternoon.

My wife and I had driven out to Tyrol Basin, near Mt. Horeb, in the morning for a half a day of skiing and I really didn't want to quit when the time came, so I decided on just one more run, and then another. I stopped for a hamburger in the lodge, then took the scenic route through the hills and the countryside toward Pine Bluff and finally on into Madison.

I arrived at the office about 1:30 p.m.

When I walked into the office, Marie Dodd, a part-time switchboard operator who is from England and has a delightful British accent said,

"Happy birthday, Steve."

"Thank you," I said. "How did you know it was my birthday?"

"Oh, I just know," she answered, smiling.

The mystery soon was solved. When I got to my desk, there was a big birthday cake sitting right in the middle of it.

It had been baked by Sharyn Behnke, the editorial secretary, and it had more candles than a porcupine has quills.

I counted them. Why not? Everyone else had.

There were 48.

Four or five people began lighting the candles and some of the staff gathered around and sang "Happy Birthday."

I loved every minute of it.

As far as the world is concerned, I suppose, my 48 years have been almost totally undistinguished.

As far as I am concerned, they have been good years.

I never wanted much — a few good friends, a lot of personal freedom and just enough money to finance my needs.

Perhaps I have led a slightly misspent life, but then I never wanted to be a business tycoon or a world leader and I always have believed that you sell your freedom in direct proportion to the amount of money you make.

And I wouldn't trade a sunrise over Yosemite or a sunset in the Grand Canyon for all the money in the world. Nor would I trade a day on a trout stream, a walk in the woods, an evening in a canoe on a good bass lake, a campfire under the pines at night or even a stolen morning on a glistening-white ski hill.

No amount of money or power is worth the moments I have spent with my children while they are growing up. And you are only truly rich when your daughter looks up at you one night, with her eyes shining, and says, "I love you, Daddy."

It hasn't all been easy. There are traps and pitfalls. One misstep and you could well be lost forever.

I managed to avoid a steady job until I was 27. There were a few odd jobs in my youth. I tried my hand at barbering and, for a time, I was a railroad section hand.

Then there were four years in the Air Force where I received my education, and, later, four years at the university where I did not.

I managed to make it through the Air Force without rising above the rank of Airman 2nd Class, which is about the Army equivalent of corporal. The secret, I learned early, was to not get involved.

I call it the "Ensign Pulver theory of operation." Ensign Pulver, you'll remember, was the character in the "Mr. Roberts" story who was on a ship for a year before the captain ever saw him. In the business world it's called keeping a low profile.

The turning point in my Air Force career was one afternoon in Alaska. I was in the dayroom shooting pool when the first sergeant walked in and said, "Hopkins, don't you own a uniform?"

"Yes, sir," I answered. "Why?"

"Well, I've never seen you in one," he said.

"Sorry, sir," I answered. He wrote something in a little black book and walked out. From that moment on, I knew I was not destined to become a great military leader. I didn't like uniforms then and I don't like them now.

Eventually, the time came for me to choose an occupation.

I considered following along family lines. My father had been a barber, and I had tried that. My grandfather had been a house painter, and I had tried that, too. Neither was for me.

There had been in the family a great-uncle, named Dan, who during the Depression years ran what was politely called a house of ill repute, near Manitowoc.

Uncle Dan always wore flashy clothes and drove big cars when everyone else was wondering where their next meal was coming from. I considered following in his footsteps but decided against it for moral reasons.

I considered becoming a congressman. The work would be easy and, like they did last week, you could sneak yourself a $13,000 a year raise whenever you wanted to. I decided against that for moral reasons, too.

What I really wanted to be was a millionaire playboy, but that was out for obvious reasons. The alternative was to become a bum, but I succumbed to family and social pressures there.

So I did the next best thing. I became a newspaperman.

For 20 years I have kept a low profile and managed admirably to stay down in the working ranks of the organization. I have been secretive about my work so nobody knows exactly what it is that I do or when I'm really supposed to come and go.

For anyone above me to ask about it now would be an admission that he didn't know what was going on in his own office.

Another thing I have learned is that executives are never wrong. As far as they're concerned, an employee is doing exactly what they think he is doing.

But it has been a good life and a satisfying life and I couldn't have chosen a better profession for me. I only hope I have contributed something to it in return.

The only disappointment was early in my career, while I was still a young reporter covering the night police beat. I came in at deadline time with what I thought was a great story and ran over to the city desk shouting, "Hold the presses!"

The night city editor barely raised his eyes from the stack of copy he was reading.

He just sat there for a moment. Then he shook his head slowly and in a very quiet voice said, "We don't do that anymore."

Frustrations of a Plastic World

I was out in the country near Mt. Horeb cutting up some fire wood the other day and was about halfway through a white oak log when my chainsaw suddenly developed a strange noise and then rattled to a stop.

"Damn," I said, "it happened again."

"What happened again?" asked my dad, who was working nearby.

"The reel the starter cord is wrapped around broke," I said. "It's made of plastic."

I threw the saw in the back of the truck and we left.

The first time it happened I took it into a repair shop and the guy behind the counter looked me right in the eye and said, "It happens all the time."

"If it happens all the time," I said, "why don't they do something about it? Why don't they make them out of steel?"

"I just fix 'em," he answered. "I don't make 'em."

So I paid the $20 or $30 or whatever it was. I had been victimized.

Manufacturers will tell you it's a matter of economics. Mass-produced assembly line products keeps the costs down, they say.

Balderdash!

I think it has become an obsession with manufacturers to find out how much junk they can pawn off on the public.

Cigarets are labeled as health hazards.

There should have been a sign on my saw when I bought it that said: "This here chain saw is a piece of junk. It is made of cheap, crummy plastic parts and may be very annoying and costly."

There should be a sign on your automobile dashboard that says: "There are a lot of plastic parts in this here machine and at 30,000 miles your radio knobs will fall off."

I happen to belong to a generation that remembers when things were real, when steel was steel and when wood was wood and leather was leather.

I know there is no way you can compare the sloppy action of a plastic or fiberglass flyrod to that of a handcrafted split-bamboo flyrod.

But there are people born and raised in this plastic world who don't know the difference.

We're getting some new desks at the office. A young fellow said to me, "I hope I get one of those wooden desks."

"They aren't wooden desks," I told him. "They're phony plastic desks made to look like wood."

"Nuts," he said, "I wanted to carve my initials in it."

"If you do," I said, "all you'll get is an oil slick on your cheap plastic-handled knife."

"You mean this isn't a real bone handle?"

"Of course not," I told him.

"Shucks," he said. He walked away, disillusioned.

If plastic is better than the real thing, why doesn't it have a character of its own? Why does a plastic desk top have to look like wood? Why does a plastic knife handle have to look like bone? Why do plastic shoes have to look like leather?

I'll tell you why. It is because we are being conditioned, like Pavlovian dogs, to accept inferior products.

The same reasoning applies to other substitutes.

One day not long ago, I went through a cafeteria line and there on the dessert counter was a big tray loaded with rich-looking cream puffs.

My mouth watered. I hadn't eaten a cream puff since I was a boy. They sold for two for a nickel on Saturday mornings in my hometown bakery. That was a long time ago.

I instinctively reached for one, then I withdrew my hand. These weren't creampuffs at all. They were artificial cream puffs made with a sweet sticky goo.

They should have been labeled as such: "These here creampuffs are phonies. They are made with a sweet sticky goo to make them look like creampuffs. They don't even taste like creampuffs."

We accept substitutes blindly because we are taught at an early age to have faith in the system. Big Brother wouldn't let anything bad happen to us.

How about the saccharin controversy? Man, it looks like they might have poisoned your diet cola.

Any oldtimer could have told you that the only substitutes for sugar are maple syrup and honey, and when I say maple syrup I mean the real thing and not the kind you buy in the stores that looks like maple syrup.

Why are we always so delighted when we find something genuine?

"This is real wood," we say in surprise. "This is real leather." "This is real cream." "This is real butter."

I bought a pair of old-fashioned, hightop shoes a couple of years ago that Lyle Johnson found in the attic of Hoff's store in Mt. Horeb. They have real leather soles.

I wore them to the office and somebody said, "Hey, Hopkins, your shoes squeak."

"I know," I said, "I like the sound."

Maybe I'm only a middle-aged man caught up in a changing world and maybe I don't know what I'm talking about, but I believe progress should make things better, not worse. I believe in change, but I don't believe in change for the sake of change.

Perhaps I am a misfit and, if so, maybe I should be labeled.

How about a sign that says: "Warning — this here man with the squeaky shoes and the broken chainsaw is confused and frustrated. He may be dangerous."

Wearing Polyester Isn't Natural

I don't know when man first began covering his body, but, when he did, I suspect it was more for creature comfort than out of a sense of modesty.

It may have started, quite by accident, while he was carrying a skin slung over his shoulder and noticed it protected him from the wind and the rain.

"Hey!" he might have said in whatever primitive language he spoke, "I think I've discovered clothes." So he wrapped himself in skins and man no longer was naked.

Later, of course, man added fiber from the wool of sheep and from cotton and flax plants and wove it into cloth. Much later, he added color — and then style.

But man, for most of his history, was clothed in natural fabrics. The synthetic industry, if memory serves me, didn't begin until around World War II, when women began wearing nylon instead of silk stockings. Then came polyester and doubleknit.

Now the late 20th Century man is clothed in petroleum products. He wears doubleknit polyester leisure suits with bell-bottom trousers and he wears high-heeled plastic shoes. I think he looks uncomfortable and slightly ridiculous.

They are the kinds of clothes that don't shape themselves to the wearer — they have no character and they don't age gracefully. I suppose they serve a purpose in a throwaway society.

But I can't help but wonder what happened along the way. Who determined, for instance, that all men were shaped like slim-hipped boys (or girls) and they would all fit into tight doubleknit trousers? When men first began to try them on and discovered they couldn't get their hands into the pockets, why didn't they say, "No, we won't accept these!"?

Whatever happened to comfortable baggy old corduroy jackets, to warm wool trousers you could sit down in, to flannel shirts that were fuzzy and soft on both sides, to cardigan sweaters with leather patches on the elbows?

Whatever happened to soft leather shoes that squeaked when they were new, to wide-brimmed felt hats that were purchased unblocked and then crushed and shaped to your own taste?

Whatever happened to the winter jacket with the real sheepskin lining?

I have been engaged in a private war with the clothing industry for 10 or 15 years now. My one-man boycott has not been very effective.

A couple of years ago I set out to find a pair of roomy cotton corduroy trousers. My search was unsuccessful and it ended at a small man's store on State St.

"Where," I asked the manager politely, "can a middle-aged man who doesn't want to dress like a teenager go to find clothes?"

"That," he answered, not so politely, "is your problem. I don't care where you buy your clothes. I make my living selling to students."

I am losing my battle. The clothing industry shows no indications of reversing its trend.

I have some old clothes that have served well through the years but won't last forever.

Most of the clothes I do buy I order from L. L. Bean, a Freeport, Maine, mailorder house that got its start outfitting Maine and Canadian backwoodsmen. It is one of the few places that sells clothes that are roomy enough to move around in.

I own one suit, with a vest, that I wear on ceremonial occasions. I have one pair of old good dress shoes also reserved largely for ceremonial occasions.

The rest of the time I dress like a bum.

My favorite sport coat is a cotton couduroy jacket I bought on sale for $15 nearly 20 years ago. It's a little shapeless now, and one sleeve is ripped from an encounter with a barbed-wire fence, but it's still comfortable, and I can't bring myself to throw it away.

I have inherited some clothes, like an old wool plaid winter cap that once belonged to my wife's grandfather in Montana.

I have a few wool sweaters. One of my favorites is 25 years old. There never will be a 25-year-old leisure suit.

I have an assortment of boots, some faded old flannel shirts and a few pair of cotton wash pants.

I got to thinking about all of this the other night while I was sitting in front of the fireplace, watching my wife at work at an old spinning wheel that has been in the family for nearly 200 years.

I don't know how many feet or yards of yarn have been spun on it through the years, but it is back in action again and providing clothes for my immediate family.

My wife buys wool from farmers, washes and cards it, spins it into yarn and knits the things she no longer can find in stores — or that are priced out of range when she does find them.

There will be some fine homemade wool sweaters under the Christmas tree again this year.

Looking through an L. L. Bean catalogue the other day, I noticed the order blank was missing and I remembered I had told my wife I needed a new pair of trousers. I suspect they might be under the tree, too, come Christmas.

Maybe, just maybe, with the help of my wife and L. L. Bean, I will be able to hold out for a few more years.

I might look a little funny. But I will be warm and comfortable and I will be able to put my hands in my pockets.

We Can Still Walk If We Choose

There is, in the course of a hundred years or so, a considerable change in the world and in the way we live.

Communities grow into villages and villages into cities, and the cities sprawl out and threaten to take over the countryside.

There probably are few among us who remember the early days of the automobile, the square Tin Lizzies with the functional steel bumpers and the big, wide running boards.

Fashions change. A look through the old family album ("Did you really wear those things when you were a boy, Dad?") is testimony to that.

Most of these things seem to be cosmetic changes; they only affect the way we look and the things we look at.

But they have to do with deeper changes, too, changes within ourselves, changes in our values and in our national outlook.

The parlor stove, in the modern home, has been replaced by the thermostat on the wall. What once was a library or a den has become a family room, with the furniture arranged around a focal point called the television set. The bookshelves, laden with handsome old leather-bound books, are gone. The only visible reading material is a TV Guide on the coffee table.

Central heating, I suppose, has been a tremendous benefit to mankind. It has meant comfort at the turn of a dial. It has put an end to tedious chores, like splitting wood and hauling ashes.

But the whirring of a furnace fan does not encourage the lofty thoughts that were inspired by a roaring wood fire in the quiet of a lamp-lit room.

Television entertains us easily and, sometimes, on a grand scale, but its effect is to discourage thought and conversation. It has replaced, for too many of us, literature and poetry and art and music. It occupies our time, but, it does not add meaning to our lives.

Convenience has made life easier but not necessarily better. A jet flight from Los Angeles to New York is fast, but the experience of travel has been removed and the traveler has no sense of having traveled at all. He has missed the snow-capped mountains and the deserts and the prairies, the crossing of the wide Missouri.

He has missed, too, the leisurely hours in the dining car, the conversation in the club car, the gentle rocking of the Pullman berth, the clicking of the wheels on the rails urging him into a deep and relaxing sleep.

Consider the kitchen. The combination of instant food and the microwave oven has turned mealtime into a race. Table conversation, if it already hasn't, is fast becoming a lost art.

Sometimes we resist, just a little. "Wouldn't it be great," we say, "if we could recapture some of our lost values?"

But things have changed too fast, they have gone too far. It's too late.

Or is it?

It not only is quite possible, it is quite likely that the cosmetic changes in our lives are here to stay.

The solution lies in our ability to evaluate them. We can use technological advances to better our lives if we make them work for us, if we learn to accept and reject. The danger lies in total, unquestioning acceptance; it lies in our being not the user, but the used.

We have, still, control over our own lives and our own minds. The decisions that affect us most profoundly are still our own.

Two cars in the driveway, for example, do not commit us to riding. We can walk, if we choose.

The difficult part, now that all the modern conveniences have been offered, lies in choosing not the easiest way, but the way that in the long run is best for us.

We can learn a lesson, perhaps, from the natural world, a world which does not change. The seasons arrive and depart on schedule now as they did a hundred years ago and a hundred years before that.

Enter the woods on foot or on cross country skis now, in February, while the late winter sun is warming the snow that still lies deep on the ground. There is a feeling of timelessness there and, if you listen, you will hear the orderly ticking of nature's clock.

Stand, for awhile, in the shadow of a gnarled old oak. Touch it and feel its strength. Think about the fires and the droughts and the storms it has weathered.

Ask yourself if it would have been as strong or as sturdy had it been reared and carefully cared for in a nursery.

More Biologists Than Wildlife

There are big flights of Canada geese heading north now, a sure sign that the worst of winter is over and that spring is on the way.

The weather sense of the geese is far more accurate than the most sophisticated forecasting equipment devised by man.

And it probably is not any wonder then that man has long been determined to learn what the wild goose knows.

A little of that is all right. There are times, though, when I think we are going too far in our efforts to pick the brains of geese and of other wildlife.

It is as though we believe that understanding the direction-finding and mating instincts of the wild creatures is somehow linked to our own survival, that they might hold the key to the easy relationship with the natural world that we have lost.

All you have to do to witness a wildlife biologist in action is to turn on your televison and, with just a little channel switching, you should find a variety of programs featuring biologists tranquilizing, weighing, tagging and strapping radio transmitters on geese, grizzly and polar bears, wolves, moose, deer, eagles, hawks and falcons.

If your taste runs to underwater activity you should be able to find a number of shows featuring marine biologists tagging whales and wrestling alligators and sharks.

I assume they all are learning something, although I have yet to read or hear of a major revelation. I suspect that at least 90 percent of this kind of activity is pure entertainment, "If the people want wildlife programs, we'll give them wildlife programs."

The first time my dog was exposed to the sound of a flock of Canadas winging its way through an autumn dawn it sat right down and howled. The reaction was instinctive and, if we stop to think about it, it is equally instinctive in man.

How many of us are not stirred by this primordial sound? How many of us would be equally as stirred if the primitive honking was interrupted by the occasional beeping of a radio signal?

Last summer a young woman camping alone in the backcountry of Yellowstone National Park was killed by a grizzly. I happened to be nearby in Jackson Hole at the time and the rumor locally was that she was the victim of a previous careless camper who left a dirty, garbage-strewn campsite.

There are getting to be more and more confrontations between man and bear and I have my own theory, which could account for at least part of the problem.

A grizzly, when wounded, often will backtrack and stalk its tormentor.

Consider the park grizzlies that are constantly being harassed by man, by a continuous succession of federal, state and private wildlife experts.

When the bears venture too close to camping areas they are tranquilized by rangers and moved to the backcountry by truck or helicopter.

In the name of research they are trapped in steel cages, tranquilized, mauled, tagged, transistorized and generally poked and probed.

The last thing these animals see before the ordeal is the approach of man. The first thing they see when they regain consciousness is a group of men in blue jeans running to a 4-wheel drive pickup and speeding away.

It is quite possible that they are reminded of this indignity by the sight of the first camper who wanders innocently into their territory. I'd be mad as hell. Wouldn't you?

It's easy to sympathize with the creatures. Once, not long ago, I watched a young biologist climb up to and peer into an eagle's nest. I was hoping he would get his nose pecked.

I know legitimate wildlife biologists are positive influences on the environment. I know that if it weren't for them there would be no fish in the streams, no habitat for deer and grouse.

I am suspicious, however, of the entertainers — of the makers of films, of the writers of books and magazine articles, of all the fringe wildlife biologists at work in the backwaters of the world.

A wise man once said: "There are a lot more folk singers than there are folk listeners."

I am beginning to wonder what will happen when the biologists outnumber the wildlife.

Good Old-Fashioned Winters

I was talking to someone last week who asked what I was going to write about next.

"I don't know," I said. "I really haven't thought about it."

"Maybe," she said, "you can think of some four-letter words to describe the weather we've been having."

It occurred to me that man, among all living creatures, is perhaps the only species that has the capacity to like or dislike weather.

I have a cat that won't set foot outdoors during the winter months, but I'm sure his distaste for cold is a physical rather than an intellectual reaction.

He spends the winter months curled on a cushion in front of the fire and seems quite content. I don't know if he ever remembers summer or dreams of spring, but I doubt that he does. I suspect that he lives only for the moment and that he instinctively adjusts to winter.

Man is the only creature that fights winter. It wasn't always so. Not too long ago men were content simply to get along with winter. There were many who actually enjoyed it. It was a challenge, but the cold always was invigorating and the fire always was warm and waiting.

Winter changed the pace of life. Things slowed down. There was a welcome respite from the hectic activity that accompanied the rest of the year.

Farm life slowed almost to a standstill. The harvest was in, and the planting still was a long time away. In winter, there were only a few chores to be done.

Even the business world relaxed. There wasn't much traveling on bad days. Business could wait. Men needed time to replenish their woodpiles and for tromping paths in the snow and for stuffing cotton in keyholes and shoving rugs up against doors to keep the drafts from creeping into the house.

At night, there always was the fire and families, drawn to its warmth, would sit together and talk and read, sometimes aloud. There was time for a quiet game or two of checkers.

Winter perhaps was the quietest and most peaceful of all the seasons. And the most peaceful time of all was the period which often lasted for days after a heavy snowstorm when the world came to a halt, and we were snowbound in our own homes.

Somewhere along the line, the old-fashioned winter began to change. It was done in, I think, by central heating and the heated automobile.

We decided we would ignore winter, that we would recognize its existence only during the brief distasteful periods spent between the car and the house or the car and the office.

The temperature in an entire house could be kept at a constant 75 or even 85 degrees. The woodstove in the parlor was replaced by a television set and families gathered around it at night, but they no longer talked or listened to each other. The checker board was stored away on a closet shelf.

The automobile was demanding and people responded. Highways were sanded and salted and scraped clean. Winter travel was safe, and it was business as usual. Except for brief periods, we no longer ever were snowbound. The business world rejoiced. "Time, after all," they said, "is money."

The winter respite disappeared. "So what?" we said. "We can wear summer underwear and short-sleeved shirts the year-around. Surely that's worth something."

In our greed for material comfort, we never took the time to recognize that we had created an artificial situation based on a limited supply of oil and natural gas.

We were a nation on a drunken comfort spree and now, like any other drunk, we are waking up to a great national hangover. The party, it would seem, is over.

The moral is, of course, that we were wrong in the first place. Man was meant to live in the world and not simply on it. He is of the same substance and cannot successfully separate himself from the elements and the seasons. It would appear that the time is approaching when man will have to learn again to live in harmony with the natural world.

I, for one, have missed the good old-fashioned winter and will welcome its return.

There are things I had forgotten about it.

I welcome the return of winter woolens, from the skin out, and of caps with earflaps and of boots high enough to protect legs from the snow.

I welcome the return of the winter diet, designed to fuel the body. I'm sure the dietitians would disagree with me, but I believe there is such a thing as a meal "that sticks to your ribs."

I find that in the winter I am naturally hungry for foods like cornbread and pork sausage and fried potatoes and for homemade vegetable and potato soups. A man fortified thusly inside can have no real fear of the elements outside.

Often at night I ski in the fields not far from the house and return to warm up in front of an open fire that burns often now in the living room fireplace.

I have noticed that the whole family seems drawn to the fire on cold winter nights. The checker board is out again and it is a lot like old times.

There is a new woodstove that soon will be hooked up and burning in the den, and then we will be even less dependent on the natural gas supply for heat.

I take pride in my backyard woodpile and in my ability to contribute in a personal way to the well-being of my family. The woodpile is the result of many rewarding days spent working in country woodlots. It not only provides heat, but a feeling of mental and physical well-being as well.

If a person learns to walk in the winter, briskly enough to meet it head on, he soon finds that the heat generated by his own body is at least equal to that generated by an automobile heater. He will become healthier for it and perhaps even will find that he likes it.

It is just possible that the energy shortage signals not the end of the good life, but, instead, the beginning of an even better, more rewarding way of life.

There have been some things that have been missing from our lives. Perhaps someday we will be grateful to the energy shortage for returning us to closer family ties and fireside conversations, for replacing a mere physical warmth for a more satisfying spiritual warmth.

Perhaps we even will be grateful to it for giving winter back to us.

Thanks a Lot, Alex, Henry, Thomas

There is a considerable amount of discussion these days about an elusive something called "the quality of life."

There is the philosophy that in our eagerness to pursue materialism we have somehow lost the ability to enjoy simple old-fashioned pleasures; that somewhere along the way we have lost track of the basic ideals that form the framework of a full and satisfying life.

We race through the day; then come home at night and watch The Waltons and wish we could live more like they do.

It began when we became preoccupied with speed, when we started measuring distance in hours instead of miles.

It began when the automobile horn replaced the tinkling of the sleighbell. It began when the ringing of the telephone became a more common household noise than the singing of a teakettle. The old way of life all but ended more recently when television replaced family conversation ("Quiet! I want to hear this.")

I think the quality I miss most is a kind of serenity. It's an elusive quality, but I keep searching for it.

Occasionally I find myself demanding it. Sometimes my youngsters will start squabbling with each other and then, as youngsters will do, try to get me to participate.

"Daddy," Katy will shout, "Jayne's got my hairbrush and she won't give it back. Make her give it to me."

"Listen, girls," I tell them, "I'm getting to be an old man and I need peace and quiet. Now leave me alone and settle your own argument."

Sometimes I almost find the serenity I seek. I find it with a book by a roaring fireplace on a snowy afternoon. Sometimes. Too often the phone rings just as I am beginning to relax and unwind.

I can find it in the early morning hours on a quiet trout stream or on a lazy river in a canoe. But it's hard to be serene when you're racing half way across the state to get to your favorite trout stream and there is a storm brewing in the western skies.

I find it sometimes at my desk in the office, on a slow day when the boss is out of town. But he isn't out of town that often and it's difficult to convince him that I'm on the last half of my newspaper career and should be allowed to start tapering off.

I often find it when I write at my desk at home, working amid the familiar clutter of fishing rods, trout nets, skis and snowshoes that hang from the walls around me. But the phone rang even in the middle of this story. It was my mother. "You've been looking pretty tacky lately," she said. "I think you should buy a new suit." "Yes, mother," I assured her, "I will."

I guess I come closest to finding it working or just walking in the woods or during the long uninterrupted days and nights at my small, one-room cabin. There is no telephone or television there to distract me.

Strangely enough, I began thinking about this one day last summer on Cape Breton Island, in Nova Scotia.

Alexander Graham Bell had a summer place there, on a hilly wooded point that jutted out into a finger of the Atlantic Ocean. Not far away at the edge of the Village of Baddeck, within eyesight of his summer home, stands the Alexander Graham Bell Museum.

The museum houses originals and replicas of some of his inventions.

There are literally hundreds of photographs showing the inventor strolling around his grounds, relaxing on the porch, riding in his boats, playing with his grandchildren. He had a beard, he smoked an old curved-stem pipe, he wore knickers. He was the picture of serenity.

His den, complete with his personal effects has been re-created there. His old-fashioned, comfortable leather couch is there. His worn old corduroy jacket, with four buttons and a belt, is draped casually over one end.

There is a small desk and a comfortable chair. His pipe, unused for all these years, rests in a small tray on the desk.

Here Alexander Graham Bell sat and worked and thought and dreamed and invented. He had, remember, no telephone to distract him.

Then, one fateful day a hundred years ago, he picked up a crude instrument he had invented and summoned his assistant from another room. He said something like: "Watson, come here. I need you." Watson obediently came, and that was the beginning — or the end.

It would have been extremely frustrating to have had the only telephone in the world and nobody to call. Bell's frustration was relieved with his call to Watson and somebody has been summoning somebody else ever since.

My telephone rang exactly four times, three times since my mother called, during the two hours it took me to write this story. The doorbell rang once. My concentration was destroyed every time.

So, Alexander — and Henry Ford and Thomas Edison and whoever invented the television — I hope you enjoyed your serenity.

I know you meant well. But all I ever wanted from life was a little peace and quiet — and you guys sure took care of that.

Telephone Hunting for Mary Anne

I have this recurring nightmare.

My house is being broken into. I want the police — fast.

I pick up the telephone and dial. A voice says, "We are unable to complete your call as dialed." It offers some advice about consulting the directory. Then it says, "This is a recording."

"Help me, voice," I plead. There is no answer.

I pick up the phone book and look at the index. There is a choice. Do I want "General Information" on Page 10, "Dialing Hints" on Page 3 or "Directory Assistance" on Page 1?

I finally settle for Page 12, "How to Use Your Directory." I begin reading, frantically. The pounding on the door gets louder, and the sill begins to splinter.

I read the "Three Easy Steps for Finding a Number."

The door breaks down. I read on. "Where numbers are used in listings, they are alphabetized as though spelled out in full . . ."

My wife and children are tied to the kitchen chairs now. I'm almost finished with "Other Helpful Hints." They're coming for me. I wake up in a cold sweat.

Telephoning isn't what it used to be.

About 25 years ago, when I was in the Air Force in Alaska, I received a letter from my mother telling me my grandfather was seriously ill and had been hospitalized. I was concerned. I decided to call home.

Telephoning from Alaska at that time involved an overseas radio hookup and you had to reserve your calling time in advance.

I went to the Air Force base telephone exchange at my appointed time and placed the call. I could follow it all the way through. I heard the Alaskan operators, the radio hookup, and I breathed a sigh of relief when the Seattle operator came on the line. I listened while the call crossed the country, passing from operator to operator.

Finally, the call was connected to the exchange in Mt. Horeb, Wis. There was no answer. It was about midnight there.

"Shall I keep trying, sir?" an operator asked politely.

"Yes," I answered. "the night operator sleeps on a cot by the switchboard. He'll wake up if you keep trying."

She tried a few more times. Then I heard a familiar voice say, "Number, please." I soon was talking to my family.

Another time, in Mt. Horeb, I picked up the phone to call a friend. I gave the operator the number, and she said, "Oh, he's not home. I just saw him walk by. He's probably in the restaurant. I'll get him there for you." She did.

That was a long time ago, even before "Dial-a-Prayer."

The other night there was a note on my desk that said, "Call Mary Anne." The number to call was 1-800 plus seven other digits. I punched the numbers on my Touch-Tone phone. A voice said, "We are unable to complete your call as dialed. Please consult . . ." I hung up and tried again. Same result.

I don't know a Mary Anne. I don't know who she is or where she called from. But I thought I would make an honest try at returning her call.

I consulted my directory.

The 1-800 number is a toll-free WATS (Wide Area Telecommunications Service) call. I found the number for WATS assistance (1-800-555-1212) and dialed it.

"May I help you?" a voice answered promptly.

"Are you a recording?" I asked.

"No," the voice answered. At last I had found a real live telephone employee.

I explained my problem. "I'm sorry, sir," she said, "but we have no listing under Mary Anne."

"What about the number?" I asked. "Does it mean anything. Can you tell me at least what part of the country it might be in?"

"I can't help you. We have no listings by numbers," she replied.

She sounded friendly.

"Where are you?" I asked.

"St. Louis," she answered.

"That's amazing," I offered. "Are you the only live person in the telephone system?"

"No," she answered, "there are more of us. I'm one of three WATS operators in the country."

I was curious. There was so much I wanted to know.

"Are you happy?" I wanted to ask. "Are you married? Do you have children? Do you have hopes, dreams, aspirations? Do you ever get lonely?"

But I didn't. I knew what the answer would be: "I'm sorry, sir, but we're not allowed to give out that information."

So I only said, "Thanks for trying to help. Goodbye."

"Good night, sir," she answered. There was a sudden silence on the line.

Mary Anne, wherever you are — I tried.

The pause that refreshes — Mazomanie Wildlife Area.

Chapter Eight

FIREPLACE DAYS

A Hardscrabble Farm Full of Pride

T he colorful early autumn is almost over and another autumn is about to begin — there are signs of it now.

I'm referring to the cold rain and chill wind of autumn: the autumn of the gray skies, the freezing night, the bare landscape, the light snow that dusts the ground briefly, then is quickly blown or melted away.

I saw signs of it last weekend, at the edge of a marsh and in a meadow and along a fringe of woods.

And, when I got home, I built the first fire of the season in the fireplace.

A blazing hearthfire seems to awaken sleeping memories in a man.

There is a twisted, rusted old horseshoe on the mantel — even some of the nails are still in it — that I found on another fall day a few years ago when my father and I were walking around the old family farm in Richland County.

The farm no longer is in the family, but we had gone there for old time's sake, and asked the new owners for permission to look around.

The horseshoe was hanging on a field fence where some latter day farmer probably had put it after turning it up with a plow. But he would have been plowing with a tractor. I doubt that anyone since my grandfather has worked the land with a team.

The shoe had to have been thrown by Jerry or Bob, the team that served my grandfather so well for so many years. So I brought it home and I stood it on the mantel. Maybe it brings me good luck. I don't know. But I like it there.

When I look at it, it reminds me of my boyhood and of the old farm deep in the valley with the steep hills rising on both sides.

There was a barn that never was meant to hold more than a few cows. The milking was done by hand, much of the time in the light of a lantern that was moved from peg to peg along the wall, following the milkers from one end of the barn to the other.

There was a chicken house and a granary and a cold pure spring that provided water and cooled the milk. A small creek that started at the spring separated the barn from the house.

It's the house I remember with fondness — a house filled with activity from before sunup until long after sundown when my grandmother would fall asleep in her rocker, her reading glasses still perched on the tip of her nose, the Bible still open in her aproned lap.

The house started as a one-room log cabin, later was covered with siding, and eventually grew, room by room.

The kitchen was the center of activity. I remember the hand-pump on the sink. I can still hear it, squeaking and clattering in my mind. There was a window over the sink that looked out over the fields and down the valley and I can still see my grandfather working those fields, walking behind the team, hands gripping the plow handles, reins knotted loosely around his back.

There was a wood cooking range, and a kitchen table with a big kerosene lamp on it. There was no electricity there until sometime in the 1940s. I heard the first reports of the bombing of Pearl Harbor there, on a battery-operated radio.

To this day, I can remember the smell of that kitchen, a combination of meals simmering on the stove, of woodsmoke, and the tangy smell of fruits and vegetables stored in the entry.

I think about that farm now when I hear the repeated urgings for this nation to adopt a low-energy lifestyle and when I hear the concern expressed about the country's economic situation.

The farm was an example of a low-energy lifestyle, except for the human energy expended. There were almost no machines, everything was done by hand. The cows were milked by hand, firewood was cut by hand, butchering was done right on the farm, the hay was pitched, by hand, onto horse-drawn wagons — even the big stone that sharpened the cutting equipment was cranked by hand.

A lot of hard work and love went into the operation of that farm. A lot of pride went into it, too, and my grandfather was a proud man.

I remember him standing in front of the mailbox one day long ago, looking at his first government milk check. He tore it up: "I guess I don't want anything I didn't earn," he said.

I was born in 1929, the year the Great Depression began, and I don't remember the early years.

But I do remember my father telling me that my grandfather told him: "If things get too bad, bring your family up here. There isn't any money, but there always will be plenty to eat and a warm place to sleep."

There are a lot of memories in an old horseshoe and maybe a lesson or two.

And, that day last weekend, I took it down and hefted it and ran my finger along its rough edges. Then I placed it carefully back on the mantel.

I wondered what the future holds in store for my own grandchildren. There will be some before too many years. I wondered how they will remember me.

Armchair Adventures Are Enriching

There are days now, deep into the winter, which are among the best of the year.

They are days when the ground is covered with snow, when the wind is howling outside, when the red line of mercury is barely visible at the bottom of the thermometer.

They are days for staying inside, days for a roaring blaze in the fireplace, an easy chair, a good book.

There was a day like that not long ago, a day when I got up early, touched a match to the kindling in the fireplace, brewed a pot of coffee and settled down to read.

I am an armchair adventurer. Why not? It's harmless, it's entertaining, and it's even educational. On days like this, I have traveled to the far corners of the earth and back and I have met many interesting people along the way. Some of them have become good friends.

That's one of the good things about armchair adventuring — you can go anywhere, do anything you want; just pick something that suits your mood.

There was a day I felt like walking, so I teamed up with Colin Fletcher and, together, we walked the entire length of the Grand Canyon.

I have climbed Mt. Everest with Sir Edmund Hillary, and in the process, suffered frozen fingers and toes, altitude sickness, and many times barely escaped death from avalanches and hidden crevasses.

But that didn't stop me. A few weeks later, I tackled the first winter climb of Mt. McKinley with a party of young climbers from all over the world.

On that day not long ago I hunted big game in Africa with Ernest Hemingway. We'd been there before, but I felt like going back. It was that kind of day.

I've been an Alaskan bush pilot and I once spent an entire year in an isolated cabin in the Arctic wilderness participating in a scientific experiment.

I have canoed wild rivers. I have studied wildlife on the Artic tundra. I once spent a summer alone in the desert.

I was with Admiral Byrd at the South Pole. I have been a mountain man, trapper, Indian fighter and frontiersman.

I have hunted whales and rubbed noses with Eskimos. I've been captured by Indians and almost burned at the stake.

I've been awakened from a deep sleep by jungle drums beating their primitive message: "Death to the white intruder."

I speak a little Shawnee and a few words of Swahili, a difficult language to master.

When I finish an armchair adventure, I close the book and put it back in its place on the wall of bookshelves next to the fireplace.

And I return to my own world, a far richer man through sharing the thoughts and experiences of others.

In Search of Serenity in the Muddle

I've always yearned to lead a quiet contemplative kind of life in a neat little house, complete with bookshelves, fireplace and comfortable stuffed rocker. I would spend my time there reading, writing, listening to good music, conversing quietly with family and good friends.

So far this well-ordered life has been denied me. I live in what loosely resembles a combination of the front porch of a Maine fishing lodge and a base camp at the foot of Mt. McKinley.

The fireplace and the bookshelves are there, but I generally can't get to them without picking my way through piles of outdoor gear that are scattered all over the living room floor.

It seems like somebody always is getting ready to go somewhere.

We just get the coming-back-from-vacation pile cleaned up or the returning-from-the-weekend at the cabin mess sorted out and put away, and another pile takes its place.

Winter isn't too bad. Then there are only the snowshoes stacked against the wall behind the fireplace, the boots piled behind the door and the clothes drying on the rack in front of the fire.

A friend of mine still kids me about the winter I built an ice fishing sled in the basement and got it only as far as the living room where it spent the rest of the winter serving as a combination coffee table and foot stool. It's back in the basement now, and I never have taken it ice fishing. If my memory serves me correctly, it's now kind of a tool box with runners.

This summer's mess started soon after school was out and just continued to grow.

It began when Katy, 12, was packing for a three-day Sugar River canoe outing. She no sooner returned from that than she began assembling equipment for a week-long backpacking trip in the Kettle Moraine.

Then came Pete's 200-mile, week-long bicycle trip to the cabin in Vernon County and back, and, for a couple of days, while he was getting ready, we even had the bicycle in the living room.

The equipment from that trip has been put away, but it's been replaced by his preparations for a two-week canoe trip on the Flambeau River.

I seem to be stumbling constantly over piles of boots, back-packs, rolled-up ponchos and sleeping bags.

My own fishing trips add to the jumble, and often, wherever I can find the room, there is another pile that includes fishing vest, hip boots, waders, flyrod cases, net and creel.

My pile usually is either on the way to or from the truck and usually doesn't stay there too long. Sometimes it just stays in the truck, until Frances makes me move it.

She's not much help, either. She went shopping the other day and came home with some good bargains — a down sleeping bag, a two-man tent and two or three lightweight nylon day packs that were on sale.

And now she's added a new dimension to our living room. She's decided to edit all the movie film we've taken over the last 10 or 15 years and now the living room looks like the cutting room floor at Universal Studios.

But that's enjoyable, too, and she usually has a strip of film or two to show when I come home from work at night that will remind me of some long-forgotten incident on some long-ago trip.

We see Yellowstone again and Glacier and Yosemite and a few Christmas Eves and birthday parties and Fourth of July parades with the youngsters riding their decorated tricycles. Maybe that's worth the inconvenience of a few days of shuffling through heaps of discarded celluloid.

So I've about given up on the contemplative, well-oriented life. I guess I've adjusted to reality.

Sometimes at night, after the kids are in bed, I clear a path to the bookshelves, being careful not to step on the cat or the dog or Pete's guitar, and I pick out something that suits my mood and I sit in my stuffed rocker and prop my feet up on the nearest down sleeping bag and read.

And I look around at all these signs of activity and I think that it won't be too many years before the kids are grown up and gone and I really will live in this quiet, well-ordered house that so far has eluded me.

When I think of it in that respect, I'm not so sure it's what I want after all.

Sometimes, I guess, we don't realize just how lucky we are.

Fireside Tales for Grandchildren

The trouble with a fireplace is that it causes a man to think.

Now, you can sit in front of a television set for hours at a stretch and never think a single thought of your own.

But just try it sometime in front of a roaring blaze, especially if you're home alone and it's quiet and there happens to be a gentle snow falling outside.

Sitting by my fireplace in my favorite old wooden rocker the other morning, I got to thinking about one of my favorite quotes from the late Robert Ruark's "Old Man and the Boy" series in which the Old Man (his grandfather) says, "All a man really needs is a warm bed, a warm fire, and a quiet woman to bring him his food."

I've always thought there was a lot of truth in that, even considering the fact that it's next to impossible to find a quiet woman. But the remarkable thing about the series was the warm relationship between the sometimes cantankerous, sometimes gentle, and often devious old philosopher and his not-always-so-eager young student.

And I sat there and watched the flames licking away at the oak and aspen logs and I thought of all the stories that someday I will tell my own grandchildren.

I was lucky enough to be born a few years before the machines took over our lives so I'm going to start by telling them stories about loading hay with a wagon and a team of horses on my grandparents' hill farm in Richland County and about hitching the team to a sled in the morning to haul the milk up the road.

And I will tell them about the day one winter when we got snowbound at a farm near Mt. Horeb and how the farmer brought us the five miles or so back to town on a bright moonlit night with a team of horses and a bobsled.

When I tell them, I'll try to make them hear the creaking of the leather harnesses and the squeaking of the runners on the freshly-fallen snow. I will want them to smell the fresh hay on the bottom of the sled and feel the warmth of the buffalo robes that covered us.

I want to tell them, too, about later years, about the salmon runs I've seen on the Anchor River and the Copper River and other rivers in Alaska. I'll tell them about the friend of mine who hooked a huge King Salmon one day that took off with his line and dragged him at a dead run over the rocks and through the brush until he disappeared from view — and how this friend turned up later scratched and bleeding, his clothes torn, his rod broken, and without the salmon — and how without saying a word he rigged up another rod and began fishing again.

I'll tell them about another day I spent on the Copper River fishing for salmon with dip nets with a crew of Alaskan Indians.

I want to tell them about clam digging on the Cook Inlet Beach, near

Homer, in the bright moonlight at dead low tide, with the lanterns and driftwood fires of other clam diggers lighting up the beach for miles.

I'll tell them, too, about the time a friend and I killed two moose in a muskeg about five miles back in the Kenai Peninsula bush and how we spent about a week packing the meat out on our backs, a hundred pounds at a time.

I'm going to tell them about sleeping out on the ground in the Alaskan wilderness, taking turns guarding the camp with a rifle at night whenever there was fresh bear sign around.

And I'll tell them about the time we ran an old pickup truck out of gas on the beach near Anchor Point with the tide coming in and how the water already was over the wheels before we got it out of there.

I won't forget to bring up the cabin-warming dance one night on the Kenai attended by homesteaders from miles around, the women arriving in parkas and rubber-bottomed shoepacs and changing to dancing slippers once inside — and about a big, rough homesteader named Arne who was an artist with an axe and who turned out to be the most graceful polka dancer I've ever seen. The sound of the music and easy laughter of that night still echoes in my memory nearly 20 years later.

I'll probably bring up the time we stopped at a log roadhouse near Kenai where we wrapped our salmon catch in tinfoil and broiled it in the coals of a potbellied stove and then fed everybody there around a big rough-hewn table.

I want to tell them about the time we decided to row a rubber raft across a Cook inlet cove to save the long hike around it and came darn close to drowning when we got caught in the middle of the cove in a summer squall.

And I'll certainly tell them about the time I broke a leg in the Chugach Mountains, near Anchorage, and was rescued by a helicopter some 18 hours later after waiting it out in a small mountain cabin while three other guys hiked and skied back out for help.

And I'll tell them about a snowy weekend in another mountain cabin where, with nothing else to do, I sharpened an axe until I could shave with it.

I want to tell them so much more — about northern Wisconsin and the deer and the loons and the herons and the huge skeins of geese honking high above a marsh in the clear autumn sky, about Canadian campsites, the sunrise over the Tetons in Jackson Hole, Wyoming, and about riding a high mountain pass with a string of packhorses in Montana.

I want to tell them how brightly the stars shine in the rarefied atmosphere of a mountaintop camp.

I want to tell them these things until they say, "Oh, no, Grandpa, not again."

Then one of my daughters will say, "Let him talk. Can't you see how happy it makes him?"

Then I'll stir up the fire with my poker and I'll light my pipe and lean back in my rocker, and I'll begin: "Well, I remember the time . . ."

A March Day Says, 'Walk With Me'

There are days, now in March, that hint softly, quietly, of things to come; but there are days that remind us, too, that winter is not altogether past. The sun is warmer now, the wind has lost some of its sting, the days are growing noticeably longer. We are approaching, as the countryman might say, the beginning of the living year.

But if March is a time for beginnings, it also is a time for endings. If it is a time for anticipation; it is, too, a time for remembering.

There are warm sunny days in March that beckon to a man and seem to say, "Walk with me, my friend, there are things you must see."

And on such days I have walked along streams that were swollen with winter runoff; that had overflowed their banks, flooding marshes and lowlands with winter's refuse. I have felt, on such days, the beginnings of spring. I have waded, wet of foot, in its murky waters; I have felt its muck and mud clinging to my boots; I have felt its gentle breath and known its musky smell.

But there are days in March, too, that are not so gentle, that are neither warm nor cold, wet nor dry — foggy, damp, chilly days best spent inside, close to the hearthfire. Even a hearthfire has a special meaning in March because of the knowledge that it soon will be too warm for indoor fires, that the quiet contemplative life that is centered around the hearth soon will end, at least for a season or two.

There is a cheerful fire that warms me, even as I write now, a fire that I laid when I got up this morning, a fire that I read the morning paper and drank my morning coffee by, a fire that I later sat in front of to work.

My woodpile and I are old friends; we have been through a lot together. And every time I lay my hand on a chunk of wood and feel its rough texture, I am reminded of other days and of other places, of spring days and autumn days and even winter woodlots. I can remember the smell of freshly-disturbed humus mingled with the bittersweet smell of sawdust; I can feel the sweat on my brow, the ache in my arms. I can hear the ringing of a splitting axe striking a steel wedge; I can feel the satisfaction in a well-placed blow of the axe. I can hear the "thunk" and see a chunk of oak fall in two pieces at my feet.

I've never bought fireplace wood and as long as I'm able to cut it myself, I don't intend to. Every piece I burn has meaning because I have cut and split and hauled it by myself. When I lay a split of wood in the hearth, I know exactly where it came from.

There is good, long-burning oak from a woodlot near Blue Mounds; there is poplar from a hillside north of Barneveld; there is maple from a woods near Lodi; there is birch, cut only last fall and still green, from the backyard of a friend on the east side of Madison.

For a long winter now, this hearthfire has cheered our household. It has dried the youngsters' wet clothes when they came in from the snow and the cold, and it has warmed their fingers and toes. The dog thinks it is hers and she sleeps soundly before it.

But the real significance of a hearthfire to me is that the wood that burns there once was part of a living, growing tree, a tree that started with a seed, that later produced oxygen, helped build soil, provided shelter for birds and animals, shaded an occasional woodland wanderer, and, later, when its work was done, even was useful as fuel.

And the hearthfire is a constant reminder to me that we live in and are dependent on the living world, without which our cities of concrete and steel soon would crumble and fall.

I think of the late Henry Beston, a Maine naturalist and writer, who once wrote: "What has come over our age is an alienation from nature unexampled in human history. It has cost us our sense of reality and all but cost us our humanity . . . man has almost ceased to be man."

Perhaps now, in March and its offering of a new beginning, there is the opportunity for a renewal of our relationship with the living world. So when you hear the March wind whisper, "Walk with me," let her take you by the hand — and go.

Fireplace Provides Warmth During Storm

Man, it would appear, is not the master of his environment. He can try. He can tamper with it. He can put it to temporary use, but he cannot control it.

Man started out on this Earth cold and wet. Then, one day, he discovered fire. He used if for heat, and he no longer was cold. He used it for light and he used it to cook his meat.

The history of man since has been a history of man and his relationship to fire. Without it, he is only another animal shivering in a dark cave, intent only on his immediate survival.

Without fire, man would cease to be man.

Early man didn't take his fire for granted. He knew that a sudden rain could reduce it to a pile of sodden ashes, that a gust of wind could send it scattering into the nearby forest. He guarded it carefully.

Once man no longer was cold and his nights no longer dark, he could turn his thoughts to other things. He began to invent and he began to dream. Tools appeared, which made his life easier and gave him time. Then there was music and literature and art.

For most of all these years, man assumed the responsibility for his own heat and his own light. He cut his own wood and he piled it neatly in a woodshed or in his backyard.

Almost every home had a hearth around which all family life was centered. Each day, the lamps and lanterns were filled with oil, the chimneys cleaned and the wicks trimmed.

Electricity changed all that. Fire now was available with the flick of a finger. Man was at last free, if he paid his utility bill.

There are a few of us in which the primitive instinct still burns. We are the tenders of the open flame. Somebody has to do it.

We like food cooked over campfires. We never are happier than when we are sitting around a glowing pot-bellied stove. We have homes with central heating, but there is a big brick fireplace in the living room and a woodpile in the backyard, just in case.

We have observed the armies of men in yellow hardhats. We have watched them driving their trucks and climbing their poles. "These men are not gods," we have said. So we keep a lantern hanging in the garage and a can of fuel somewhere in a corner.

We know that only the Sun and the stars and the Earth itself are more or less permanent, and we put our faith in the natural world.

We know that all of man's creations are, after all, no more permanent or durable than sand castles perched on a tide-swept beach. We have witnessed storms and floods, tornadoes and hurricanes, earthquakes and tidal waves — and we know this to be true.

We seldom get a chance to say, "I told you so."

But it took only a three-day ice storm to put much of Wisconsin and the Midwest out of business. It took only three days for the storm to begin disassembling the network of powerlines on which we have come to depend.

It took only three days to turn the clock back 100 years.

I write this on Friday morning in front of a roaring fire, the only place in the house where it is warm.

We have been without electricity for almost 24 hours. It has been an enjoyable 24 hours, an adventure.

We spent Thursday night bathed in the glow of candlelight and, when it was time for bed, we slept in sleeping bags on the living room floor in front of the fireplace.

The fire went out during the night and I was awake for a long time listening to the wind whistle in the chimney.

Frances and I were up at first light to get the fire started again. She laid the base on the hearth while I took the ax and went outside to split a supply of wood. There was something that felt good and right about working at a woodpile in the cold, gray dawn.

Breakfast was made on a campstove on the kitchen table and, after breakfast, the kids took turns warming their clothes and dressing in front of the fire. It was a familiar scene somehow, a scene that has been played in wood-heated homes throughout the history of man.

We are ready for a seige of powerless living. Dry wood has been stacked in the garage. Perishables have been removed from the now useless refrigerator and stored outside, in the cold.

We are ready to hold out for days, but I suspect the power will be back on within at least another day. I'm not sure I will welcome its return. I kind of like tending my own fires.

The family building the cabin.

Chapter Nine
PAGES FROM THE CABIN JOURNAL

A Cabin and Some Country

W e had a visitor at the cabin not long ago, a man from the city, one of those nervous fussy men who likes things neat and orderly.

He came in out of a cold, spring drizzle and stood by the stove and warmed himself while we chatted. He looked around the cabin, at the unfinished door and window frames, at the still-exposed 2-by-4s and ceiling rafters. I knew what he was thinking.

"I suppose," he remarked, "you will finish it someday."

"It is finished," I said. "It has been finished for more than five years now."

"Oh?," he answered. He couldn't resist commenting that a little paneling would "dress it up."

"A little paneling," I told him, "would make it look like a motel lobby."

The cabin is not a fancy place. It is, in fact, exactly what it was intended to be — a shack in the woods.

It is a sturdy building and it serves my purpose. It keeps me warm and dry. It does not object to my muddy boots.

I come here not to dust and clean or to build and paint. There is no lawn to care for. The woods starts at the cabin door.

My wife is a harvester of woodland crops, a hunter of mushrooms, a picker of berries and wild grapes and asparagus and watercress. The cabin does not demand her subservience. She is free to roam.

I, too, am free to walk the wooded hills and the meadows of Salem Ridge — to do nothing more important than observe the changing of the seasons. I am free to watch and to listen and to wonder.

It is not good, I think, for a man to be too long in the city. There are distractions and noises there that dull the senses. There is the danger he will forget how to listen to the natural world.

Spring has its own sound, as do the other seasons.

There is the crisp, rustling sound of autumn, the sound of dry leaves blowing in the wind.

Winter is the howl of the north wind, the crunching of snow under booted feet.

The summer sound is the incessant droning of millions of tiny winged insects.

The sound of spring is the sound of running water, the trickling of melting snow, the soft patter of spring rain, the rushing of flood-swollen rivers and streams.

There is water now in the dry creekbed that runs past the cabin. It is a babbling brook, for a while at least, and the sound of spring greets me just outside the cabin door.

There is the spring sound, too, of the cardinal that sings to me from a hillside treetop when I go to the woodpile in the early morning.

It is raining lightly this morning when I leave to follow the creek up the valley to its source. I put on an old jacket and pull my hat brim down to keep the rain off my glasses.

The stream is shallow and I walk sometimes on either side of it and sometimes in it, depending on where the footing is best.

I have not walked far before three ruffed grouse explode almost from underfoot. There is nothing more startling than the sudden whirr of a grouse taking flight. Every woodsman knows the sound. Certainly, every grouse hunter knows it.

There are signs along this spring creek that other woodland creatures have discovered it, too. I wonder if they enjoy this seasonal bonanza as much as I do. I hope so.

Signs of spring are everywhere. Sap buckets hang from the sugar maples deep in the woods. Maple syrup, fresh from the spring run, sweetened our own breakfast this morning.

How good it is to tramp the woods on this spring day.

How good it is, in any season, to feel the warmth of the Sun, the chill of the rain, the sting of the wind — to be free to walk the Earth and climb its hills and explore its woods, to gaze up at its mountains and down into its canyons, to wade its waters, and to paddle the waters that are too deep to wade.

How good it is to be alive.

My morning walk ends, still in the rain, on the hilltop above the cabin. I am wet and a little cold. Through the trees, I can see the cabin roof and the smoke rising from the chimney.

I feel a momentary twinge of pity for the city visitor who concerns himself with paneled walls; a man destined to spend eternity in a neatly-paneled box who chooses to spend his lifetime in one, too.

I walk on, down the steep hillside, through the soft wet humus, to my shack in the woods — eager now for the warmth and comfort I will find inside.

March Rain Forecasts Spring

It's a raw, rainy March day, a good day to be inside the cabin looking out.

A strong wind blows and swirls last year's dead leaves up through the valley. I suppose there is a reason for a spring windstorm; it's a kind of house cleaning, nature's way of sweeping out the woods in preparation for the new summer growth.

I have a good fire going in the stove and, inside the cabin at least, it is warm and dry. Sudden gusts of wind affect the draft in the stove, and the stove pipe howls and crackles.

I had planned to take an axe to a couple of trees today — one for firewood and one to leave for a grouse drumming log, but, while I'm thinking about it, the rain starts again, softly at first, then harder, driven up against the windows by the wind. The tree-cutting can wait for a better day.

Today is a good day for reading and for making notes in the Cabin Journal.

By mid-afternoon, I get a little restless. When the rain lets up, I put on a waterproof parka and head for the woods. I haven't been to the cabin for a couple of weeks and I'm anxious to see what changes the coming of spring has brought.

I hang a camera around my neck and zip the parka over it to keep it dry. I walk up the creek where deer have walked not long before. The rain has not yet erased their tracks in the wet sand.

The creek is running high now and faster than usual, and I head for a spot where the water tumbles over wide limestone ledges in a series of miniature cascades. I want to take some pictures here, but the light is bad. I try a few shots anyway.

I take the long way back to the cabin, a circular route up over the hill and through the woods. A patch of wildflowers in a hillside clearing catches my eye. They are hugging the ground as if withdrawing from the cold and the rain. Their petals are not yet open, but the first warm breeze, the first touch of sunshine will do it. I examine them on hands and knees and find they are white violets (incognita).

Farther into the woods I stop to photograph a woodpecker tree. Nearby, at the base of another tree, I spot some bloodroot just ready to blossom. I lay on my stomach in the soft, wet humus and try to photograph these.

Frances joins me in the woods and we climb the hill behind the cabin — up across the big meadow and back down into the woods on the other side, through tangles of brush and briars and in and out of the deep ravines.

I notice the sumac, and, here and there, some poplar shoots are spreading into the meadow. Someday they will take it over, the advance guard of a new forest growth.

I wonder — if man ever disappears from the Earth and then reappears, millions of years from now — if somebody, someday will want to clear the meadow again. I decide not to worry about that.

Back at the cabin, in the waning light of day, I take the gas lanterns to the porch and fill them. We need them to light our way outside at night.

During supper, we listen to the news and then music on the radio, and it seems strangely pleasant and relaxing in this television age.

We turn in early at the cabin. I stay up and read awhile after everyone else has gone to sleep; then I put a chunk of wood in the stove and turn in myself.

I wake up sometime during the night and notice that the wind has stopped blowing. The only sounds are the crackling of the stove and the soft patter of a gentle rain falling on the roof.

I lie awake and listen for a long time.

A Jaunt in the Morning

(From the Cabin Journal) — The first sounds I hear this morning are made by my father who is up early and starting a fire in the cabin stove.

I lie, buried under a warm pile of wool blankets, and listen while he crumples up an old newspaper and stuffs it into the stove. I hear him add the kindling and touch a match to it and I hear the metallic clang when he closes the stove door. Soon the flames are crackling in the stove pipe.

I get up to join him and stand close to the stove, absorbing its heat while I dress.

It is light, but not yet full light.

I walk to the porch and light my pipe and watch the Sunrise. When the first rays rise above the eastern hills I turn to Dad and say, "Let's go for a walk."

We take a couple of jackets from their pegs on the wall behind the door and start out, down the lane to the road.

There is no hurry today — no appointments, no deadlines. There is only the morning and the woods.

We walk in silence, listening to the country sounds.

The woods is filled with the singing of early-rising birds. There is a flock of goldfinches in a tree near the roadside, their black and yellow feathers shine brilliantly in the morning sunlight. They greet us as we near — ti-dee-di-di, ti-dee-di-di.

We hear the incessant tapping of the woodpeckers, the bold cawing of the crows. An owl hoots from the hillside. It is one of the first sounds we hear this morning and one of the last we heard the night before.

We walk a mile or so down the road and stand, leaning on the railing of an old iron bridge, and watch a small brook dance over its rocky bed below. We listen to its song.

A fat woodchuck ambles across the road nearby, then it sees us and scrambles for cover.

I am glad it's only May. I find myself eagerly anticipating the summer and remembering other summers and other summer mornings. I wonder how much memory contributes to anticipation.

I remember other mornings on north woods lakes, with the loons calling and the ducks flying low overhead. When I think of them I can feel the morning chill and see the wisps of mist drifting across the top of the water just before the Sun breaks through and burns it away.

I remember mornings in the high country and the trout leaping in the mountain lakes, and the smell of the pines and the feel of the needles underfoot when you walk down to the creek for a pail of water.

I remember summer mornings in the Grand Canyon, and waking up to the heat of the desert and the sound of a string of pack mules coming down from the rim on the Kaibab Trail, the scuffling hooves and the creaking harness leather and the occasional crisp command of the mule skinner.

I remember summer mornings on the North Atlantic with the tide coming in, and the sound of the gulls and the tangy smell of a salt water marsh and the feel of the deck of a fishing boat rolling gently on the swells of the Gulf of St. Lawrence off Prince Edward Island.

Dad and I return to the cabin for breakfast, and, after breakfast, Frances and I set off up the hillside for another morning jaunt.

The hillside is covered with spring flowers, with trillium and jack-in-the-pulpits and Mayapples. I poke around the underbrush with the tip of an old cross-country ski pole I use for a walking stick, looking for morels as we climb.

Frances takes the hilltop, along the edge of the woods. I traverse the hillside through the woods.

I discover a blackened path, maybe a hundred yards square, that has been burned up into the woods. The undergrowth has been burned away and the based of the trunks of the trees have been blackened, but they are leafing out and don't seem to have been damaged.

"Frances, come here!" I shout. "We've had a forest fire!"

We follow the blackened path down to the road and decide it must have started when someone threw a lighted cigaret from a car into the dry leaves in the roadside ditch.

We later found that it had happened a couple of weeks before, while we were away, and that the La Farge Fire Department had been called to put it out.

We climb the hill again and find a few morels in the old apple orchard at the edge of the hilltop meadow.

We cross the meadow and walk deeper into the woods on the other side. We find more morels here and there, usually popping up through the dry leaves not far from the base of a recently dead elm tree. Soon we have enough for dinner.

It is Mother's Day and we have a dinner of ham and morels, fried in flour and butter, and fresh asparagus picked from along the country roadsides the day before.

The Sun is high in the sky now, and it has warmed the cabin porch where we sit and talk after dinner.

I feel very lucky to be here. It is good, in May, when the summer is just beginning.

Fences and Good Neighbors

In New England, in the days of stone fences, farmers would meet in the spring to walk their fencelines, one on each side, to replace stones dislodged by frost or by hunters.

This inspired Robert Frost, in 1913, to write a poem called "Mending Wall," in which his neighbor and fencing partner maintained that "good fences make good neighbors."

Frost disagreed. "Isn't it where there are cows?" he asked. "But here there are no cows. Before I built a wall, I'd ask to know what I was walling in or walling out."

Frost was saying fences often are built where there is no need for them.

There is another kind of wall that can cause problems between neighbors — the "No Hunting or Trespassing" sign. Breaks in this wall are not easily repaired.

A few years ago I was a newcomer, an outsider, in a Vernon County valley in the Kickapoo Hill Country of Wisconsin. There were neighbors who had lived there for years, many whose families had been there for generations.

I started to build a cabin that would take up 412 square feet of space. It would scarcely make a dent in the 40 acres that surrounded it.

I stood there one spring morning, hammer in hand, and watched a dilapidated old car pull into the lane. Two old men in slouch felt hats and bibbed overalls got out. They kind of looked around the cabin. They didn't talk much.

There was a little conversation about the weather. They finally got around to mentioning that there was ginseng on the hillsides there, which they usually hunted and picked in the fall. They asked if I was going to post the land. I said, "No. Go ahead and use this place like you always did." They were laughing and waving when they left.

A neighbor lad, Phil Allen, and a young friend stopped by later. I hadn't yet met Phil then. They said they had a good deer stand on a hillside on my 40 and wanted to know if I was going to post it. I said, "No. Go ahead and hunt."

Two grouse hunters (I think they were teachers from town) asked the same question. Again the answer was "No." They promised to show me some good fishing holes in return. I haven't seen them since and I assume they've moved on to other schools.

There were others — the mushroom hunters and the farm wives who knew about the berry patch at the other end of the 40 where the old log cabin stands. The answer was always, "No. You've been here longer than I have. Consider this land yours. Treat it like you always have."

I never have had cause to regret not posting my land.

The cabin has stood for about five years. It never has been broken into. Nothing on my property ever has been damaged.

Sometimes, going up there in the winter, I have seen footprints in the fresh snow, footprints of hunters who have walked up the lane, past the cabin, and on into the woods. Never have these footprints led to a door or a window. Apparently nobody has even stopped to try to peek inside.

I know my close neighbors do, and I have the feeling that even others who use the land are helping to keep an eye on things while I'm away.

No man really can own land. He can, at best, be a kind of caretaker. Woods and meadow and lakes and streams were put on this earth to be used and enjoyed by all.

No man has a right to deny another a view from a hilltop.

If he owns a hilltop, and meets a stranger there and orders him to leave, he has made an enemy.

If he welcomes him, and if they sit and enjoy the view together, he will have made a friend.

"Good fences make good neighbors?"

Except for protecting crops and livestock, good neighbors don't need fences.

In the Heat of Summer

It always is a pleasant surprise to return to the cabin and discover the changes that have taken place while we were away.

We have been away this time for more than a month — far away, in Colorado, Arizona, Utah, Wyoming and Montana.

Nature has been busy during our absence. The woods has reached its full summer growth, and when we arrived here yesterday the cabin no longer was visible from the road; it seemed almost to have retreated into the hills.

The brush had grown up around the gate post and I had to hunt for the padlock that secured the chain. The weeds were taking over the lane. We drove in slowly, parting a sea of Queen Anne's Lace as we went. A deer that had been resting near the cabin leaped up and bounded away.

There is a path through the woods, from the end of the lane to the cabin, and now it was lined with ripe, red raspberries.

Wasps had established a summer housing development under the eaves, and they buzzed angrily around me while I fumbled with the lock on the back door.

I didn't blame them. I was the intruder. Wasps know nothing of property rights, of deeds and abstracts and such.

It is pleasant, too, to walk into the cabin, after an extended absence, and find that it has not changed.

It is only a one-room shack, but it is well-built and secure from winter winds and summer storms. The woods grows up to the door, but it does not reach inside.

I willingly share the outside with the other creatures, but the inside is mine, and I guard it jealously. The occasional wasp that finds its way in here is disposed of quickly.

There is a feeling, on returning after a long absence, that time had stopped while we were gone. Everything is in its place, just as we left it.

There are some winter clothes hung over a rafter above the stove. They were tossed up there one day last winter to dry, after a wet and cold cross-country skiing outing. They will remain there until they are needed again next winter.

Even a book I was reading is still open and upside down on the big oak table, marking the place where I left off more than a month ago.

It takes only a few minutes for us to reestablish our presence. We open the windows and the doors to capture whatever breeze there might be in

August.

We set the chairs out on the porch, bring in the sleeping bags, the food cooler and the water jugs. We are, for the time being at least, home.

August is not my favorite month here. I don't dislike it, it's just that it's not my favorite. I much prefer the winter and the quiet cold, even the raging snowstorms.

I like the spring, when the creeks are full and the spring rains pound on the cabin roof at night.

I like the fall and the crisp autumn mornings and the color that is in the woods in October.

We come here only occasionally in the heat of summer. Most of the activity is confined to the cabin and the porch. Outings are confined to blackberry picking expeditions on the hilltop fringes of the woods or to long easy walks along the winding country roadsides.

But deep in the valley, even the August nights often are cool. The porch thermometer tonight is right on 50 degrees, and there is a small kindling fire in the cabin stove — just enough to take the damp chill out of the air.

The night is clear. The stars seem almost within reach, just above the treetops, and the moon, in its first quarter, drifts quietly through the sky.

The stars could well be tiny jewels in a gigantic clock that tells time, not by the minute or the hour, but by the seasons. It is possible that time, as I conceive it, does stop while I am away. It occurs to me that, if I left here now and didn't return until next August, I would be aware of no changes at all.

I'm not going to do that. But it's something to think about.

Only Man Has Choices

Man, unlike the other creatures that inhabit the Earth, has the capacity to choose what he will do with his days.

There is work that needs doing in my valley here, but I keep putting it off. The cabin woodpile, for instance, has shrunk and I must soon begin the process of making more wood if I am to be warm and comfortable on the fall and winter days that are not far away.

I should climb, brush hook and axe in hand, to the hilltop and begin cutting back the sumac and aspen shoots that are threatening to take over the meadow there.

The work will get done, on later cooler September days and perhaps crisp clear golden days in October.

But right now I choose to walk and observe the changes that are taking place on the land as summer gradually gives way to autumn.

The hornets that live in a paper nest under the cabin eaves don't have this freedom of choice. The workers are busy these days flying in and out of the nest to gather provisions for the community inside.

They have much to do now and time is running short. Most of them will die with the approach of winter, but they will have done their work and the species will go on.

I walk among the wildflowers that grow on the roadside and along the lane — the woodland sunflowers, fleabane, goldenrod, bellflowers, and Queen Anne's Lace. I inspect the wild grape vines that are climbing the roadside trees.

I disturb an occasional bumblebee. They, too, are racing the killing frosts that will touch, first in the deep valleys, before too many nights are past. They ignore my intrusion and go on about their work.

At night the cutworm moths (the common millers) cling silently to the outside of the porch screen, drawn by some primeval force to the light inside. Sometimes, when the screen door is opened, one will slip inside and circle the hissing gas lantern on the porch table until, finally, it flies too close and loses its life. Unlike the industrious hornets and bumblebees, the existence of the moth seems to be aimless, without purpose. I think about the lives and struggles in the insect world and wonder if there are lessons there for man.

Am I, I wonder, a bumblebee or a moth?

I decide it's time for me to get to work — before the winter comes and I'm caught with my woodpile down.

Autumn is time of change

Today is the first day of autumn and I am here at my cabin in the Kickapoo hills to observe it.

There must be more important things to do, but I can't think of any. It somehow seemed necessary that I be here now.

I guess I am among the self-appointed observers of seasonal changes. Somebody has to do it.

The encyclopedia tells us fall is the season which follows summer and precedes winter. Astronomically, it begins with the autumnal equinox, when the Sun enters Libra.

There is more to it than that. It is a season of subtle changes in the natural world.

There have been light frosts in the valley at night, and the summer's growth has begun to wither and die.

The woodsmoke rises straight up from the chimney now, into the crisp morning air.

The poplars along the edges of the woodlots are turning from green to gold. There are touches of red on the hillsides. The bittersweet berries seem just a little brighter. The remaining grapes on the vines are aglow with the first touch of frost.

The age-old rhythms of life and death and rebirth continue, oblivious to man's efforts to interfere. Perhaps that is the beauty of it — that nature is not at all concerned with the preservation of man.

Some of us find it hard to accept, but man is no more or less important in the total scheme of things than the oak tree or the squirrel.

We are, by design, an endangered species. There were billions of autumns, witnessed only by flying reptiles and giant ferns, before man arrived. There will be that many more after man has disappeared from the Earth.

In the meantime, it is enough just to be here and watch and wonder and marvel at it all.

Man is a funny creature, if you think about it. The city man, particularly, dislikes winter. He begins girding himself for battle in the fall and, in a couple of months, he will set forth, armed with plows, shovels and snowblowers, intent on ridding the Earth of ice and snow.

Man, who springs from the elements, has bridged almost every river and stream on Earth. For all his lofty hopes and dreams and aspirations it would seem that man, in the final analysis, is most concerned with keeping his toes warm and his feet dry.

I think when we deny the natural world we somehow are denying our own beginnings, our role in the natural order.

I had a great-great-grandfather, Harvey Gillingham, who came from Ohio to settle in Richland County in 1851.

This morning, on an impulse, I drove to what is now the community of Gillingam, turned onto a town road and headed back into the hills. I had never been there before. Nobody told me the way.

I came to an old farmhouse. There was a spring pond in the front yard. A trim gentleman of about 70 years was laying tomatoes out to ripen on a low, flat shed roof near the road. I slowed down. The name on the mailbox read: "Gillingham."

I got out and introduced myself, and he said, "You must be the fellow who writes for the newspaper. I was wondering if we'd ever meet."

His name, he said, was Sanford Gillingham. In only a few minutes, I felt I had known him for a long time. In a way, I suppose, I had.

Sanford's home, it turned out, is the original homestead. More than a century ago, Harvey Gillingham stood by the same spring and decided he would settle there. It has stayed in the family for all these years.

Driving back here, to my own place, I felt a strange sense of peace and belonging, an awareness of my own role in the order of things.

My family has been observing the coming of fall in the Kickapoo hills for 125 years. I wonder if I have inherited some instinct, if I was drawn here not by my own choice, but by design.

This afternoon I walked the rugged hillsides, just as Harvey did before the Civil War, just as Sanford does now.

I traveled slowly through the woods, stopping frequently to sit and to watch.

The squirrels were harvesting the hickory nuts and acorn crop and did not seem too offended by my presence. They would withdraw to a tree trunk to scold, but they did not flee in terror.

I flushed three ruffled grouse and watched them disappear through the treetops.

I waded a creek and got my boots wet. I filled my own pockets with hickory nuts and apologized to a squirrel watching from a tree not far away.

"Look," I said, "You'll only forget where you put them anyway." He chattered something I didn't understand in reply.

Satisfied that the woods, and the world, were in order, I returned to the cabin.

I am writing now on the front porch, in the last slanting rays of the early autumn Sun. The warmth is fading along with the Sun and there will be frost again tonight. The fire will feel good.

I suppose this has been an unproductive day in terms of the modern definition of production.

But there are things that can't be measured or weighed, or bought or sold.

I watched a golden leaf fall to the ground today, but I knew there would be another to take its place in the spring. And I knew that even though leaves fall and die, the tree will survive.

Maybe there is hope, after all, for man — if we learn before it is too late that survival is linked not to the golden leaf, but, instead, to the gnarled and tangled roots buried deep in the ground.

The Joy of a Walk in Winter

There is a kind of joy in starting a new winter day in a cabin deep in the woods and the first thing I notice this morning is the silence. There is not a sound anywhere, not even from the stove which quit snapping and crackling sometime during the night.

It is warm and comfortable in my sleeping bag, but I do not linger there long this morning. I unzip it and sit up, and I am wide awake before my feet touch the floor.

It snowed a little during the night, and I look out of the cabin window at a fresh white world. The sun is just beginning to rise above the eastern hills. The thermometer on the porch reads 8 degrees below zero.

I stuff some paper and kindling in the stove and light it and soon have a good blaze going. I put the coffee pot on. There will be steak and eggs later, when the cabin is warm and Frances and the girls get up, but coffee will do for a start.

I turn on the radio to catch the early morning news and stand close to the stove to dress. I suppose there is something in the news that is important, but it does not interest me. It seems to concern a different, remote world. It does not touch me here.

I pull on a set of longjohns, wool pants, a flannel shirt, a heavy sweater, two pair of wool socks and lace on a pair of leather boots. I am ready for anything the weather, inside or out, has to offer.

I settle down with my coffee and a book and wait for the stove to do its work.

My reading is interrupted by the sound of a car driving into the lane, and soon there is the sound of heavy boots stomping off snow on the porch. I know by the sound that it is neighbor Theron Phillips stopping by for his morning visit. This morning he is on the way to help a son-in-law cut firewood, but he is concerned that my car might not start.

"I think it will," I tell him "but I suppose you'll worry about it if we don't try it."

We walk out to the car. It sputters once, then roars to life. The cold, outside air is brisk and invigorating, and, when Theron leaves, I grab an old ski pole I sometimes use for a walking stick from the porch, motion for the dog to come along and start the long climb up a steep hillside near the cabin.

I have climbed this hill many times, and I never tire of it. This morning, in the new unbroken snow, it is like being alone in a strange new world.

There is an old wagon road near the top of the hill, and I am perspiring by the time I reach it. I lift my earflaps from my ears and unzip my jacket and follow the wagon road to a fence that runs along the edge of the thick woods.

Tracks of deer and field mice and squirrels along the fenceline tell me I am not the first creature to be up and about.

There was a time I would have crawled under the fence, through the snow, but the idea doesn't appeal to me this morning. I walk along the fenceline, looking for an easy place to cross.

I am half-way through the fence, with one leg on one side and one on the other, when a deer leaps up ahead of me and bounds away through the trees, leaving a fine cloud of fresh snow blowing in its wake. The dog gives chase but gives up shortly and comes back, panting happily when I call her.

The Sun's rays are slanting through the trees now, and I walk through a winter world lined with patches of bright and shadow.

I follow a familiar trail through the woods and end up on the other side, high on a hilltop meadow. I brush the snow from a stump at the edge of the meadow and sit here to light my pipe and rest.

From my lofty perch I can see the deep valleys and the tops of other ridges that surround me. I can see the smoke rising from chimneys of farmhouses in the distance.

I have read the predictions that the world is in danger of becoming so overpopulated there will only be a few feet of space for every living person. The danger does not seem great here and now. But, if I were around when it happened, I think I might choose this spot.

I walk on, circling the woods until I cross another meadow. Then there is a steep drop through a patch of pine woods to a deep creek bottom. I cross the frozen creek and climb the steep bank on the far side. It takes both hand and footholds to negotiate the bank. I can hear my heart pound from the exertion, and it is a pleasant sound.

There are two more hills to climb and descend before I end up on a town road about a mile away from the cabin. The last mile is a pleasant stroll. The cabin is warm when I return. I throw another chunk of wood on the fire and wash up for breakfast.

His boots know no concrete sidewalks

There's a man I know that I wish I could be more like.

I think of him every now and then, when I'm sitting in the office staring out the window at the cold, gray concrete parking ramp across the street.

This man, now in October, lives in a world of burnished gold and brilliant red.

He has few bills to pay, no deadlines to meet. He doesn't have a care in the world.

I saw him again just last weekend. He was sitting on a hillside up in the Kickapoo Valley, in Vernon County.

He was wearing an old Stetson hat to keep the briars and prickly ash from scratching up his bald head. The pockets of his ancient corduroy shooting jacket were stuffed with shotgun shells, hickory nuts, wild apples, and pipe tobacco.

A 12-gauge shotgun was cradled across his lap. He'd flushed a half-dozen grouse already that morning, but hadn't shot at any. Somehow it hadn't seemed right to kill on a day like this, a day so alive with sunshine and vivid color. He wondered if there was any good time to kill; he'd been thinking a lot about that lately.

He stood up now and motioned to his son, a 13-year-old carbon copy of himself who was sitting nearby.

"Let's make a swing down along the creek and cut up the hill into that patch of woods on the other side of the fence," he said quietly.

"Okay," the boy replied.

Together they dropped down the steep bank to the creek, boot heels digging up clumps of humus where they kicked them in to slow their descent.

The stream here flows fast and clear, dropping over occasional small rapids into a series of clean, leaf-lined pools. They stopped by one of the pools to drink and to splash a little cool water on their faces.

A half-mile downstream they climbed out of the ravine and entered a lush woods. A slight breeze came up and they were showered with gold sugar maple leaves.

A fox that had been hiding in a clump of brush made a noisy break for freedom and the man and the boy jumped back in alarm; then they laughed at themselves for their foolishness.

They picked some apples from a tree. Tracks around it told them the deer had found it, too.

This man lives simply, in a cabin in the woods. In the heat of summer, he is cooled by woodland breezes. Glowing white oak coals in a big Michigan stove warm him in the fall and winter. His booted feet know no concrete sidewalks, only the soft feel of forest trails.

His friends are farmers, hill people. And they sit on the ground or lean on tractor fenders and puff on their pipes and talk about crops and government and taxes and hunting and the price of fuel oil.

He has time for his family; his wife, son, and two little girls. They walk in the woods together, or up the winding gravel road that runs through the valley. They pick blackberries and wild grapes and walnuts. They listen to bird songs.

One night last weekend they stood in a clearing in the woods in the crisp night air and counted stars that were hanging in a sky so clear that the Milky Way looked almost within reach.

They went back to the cabin and warmed themselves before the fire. At bedtime, the man walked to a shelf of books and pulled one out. Then, sitting in a comfortable chair by the stove with his family gathered around him, he began to read aloud a story about a boy and a raccoon.

I'd like to have stayed around longer, but the weekend eventually faded away and it was time for me to go. So I said goodbye to my friend who lives in the woods and I climbed into my car and drove back to the city.

I miss my friend when I'm in the city, but he won't come back with me. He claims the confusion and the noise and the concrete don't agree with him.

Besides, he has his own life to live, and I'll be seeing him again soon anyway.

I wish I could be more like that man, but I just don't seem to have the time.

Gloria De Haven.

Carolyn Pflasterer

Chapter Ten

AND FINALLY

Life, Sometimes, Is Like the Movies

I once had a friend, who, during the few years he lived there, saw every movie that played at the Strand Theater in Mount Horeb.

I wasn't far behind, nor were most of the others who were growing up in a small town during the 1930s and '40s.

Movies, for us, were the bridge between middle America and the rest of the world and it didn't matter that the world we witnessed on the silver screen was a little distorted and often over-glamorized. It was the world we knew we would inhabit, someday, when we were old enough.

There wasn't much excitement in the midwestern small town of the '40s except for a week during the summer while the Brooks Tent Show was in town or for a few days in the fall during the annual Harvest Festival when the wire walker strung his gear high over Second Street. There were some tense moments for us youngsters while we followed him around prior to showtime, watching him carefully test the wind.

But these were only occasional diversions and the real path to adventure was a slightly worn red carpet that led from the movie theater box office to front row center. There, at the broad end of a beam of light, we watched our youthful dreams unfold.

There was travel, there was adventure, there was music and singing and dancing and most of all, perhaps, there was romance.

There was an opening night three times a week and we observed these opening nights with ceremony befitting the most lavish of Broadway musicals.

It was traditional to arrive a little early and hang around outside, waiting until a small group was gathered so we could go in together. While we waited, we painstakingly examined the coming attractions posters that were tacked inside glass cases on the front of the theater.

Eventually, we would saunter casually inside, stopping in the lobby long enough to pick up a supply of popcorn and Milk Duds before we claimed our seats and waited restlessly for the movie to begin.

What a world the movies opened to us. How else could a country boy get a glimpse of a waterfront bar in Hong Kong, the plush interior of a penthouse apartment in Manhattan, a ski lodge in Sun Valley, a monastery in Tibet, the inside of a C-47 flying the Burma Hump, the Broadway stage, the inner workings of a Los Angeles newsroom?

There was a time, then, when the corridors of Alcatraz were as familiar to me as the hallways of the Mount Horeb public school.

The actors were larger than life. John Wayne. Jimmy Stewart. Cary Grant. Gary Cooper. Clark Gable. Spencer Tracy. Henry Fonda. Tyrone Power. Fred Astaire. The handsome and dashing Errol Flynn. Modern movie actors and the common television variety pale by comparison.

They taught us everything from Indian fighting to tap dancing, they taught us wit and sophistication, they influenced our dress and they taught us how to kiss without bumping noses.

And if we idolized the men and strove to pattern ourselves after them, it was the actresses who really held our attention.

We learned about women from Ida Lupino and Susan Hayward and

Betty Grable and Ann Sheridan and Barbara Stanwyck and from June Allyson and Mitzi Gaynor and Virginia Mayo and Ann Miller — and from Gloria DeHaven who for a few years was the secret love of my young life.

But movies end and dreams do not stand up well to the harsh light of reality. So it is with the innocence of youth.

We grow up and we discover that waterfront bars serve warm beer in dirty glasses, that the inside of a C-47 is a cold and lonely place, that the life of a newspaperman is not at all like Bogart played it.

But even in the adult world, the magic that once surrounded the stars still exists. I have seen three of them, in real life, in the years since the Strand Theater days and I have felt the magic every time.

I once came to work two hours early to get a glimpse of Rhonda Fleming who was doing some promotion work in Madison. I wasn't disappointed.

Quite a few years ago, when I was stationed at an Air Force base in California, Sterling Hayden walked into the hangar where I was working to get a drink of water. He said, "Hello." I just stared at him, wide-eyed, and mumbled something unintelligible in return.

And I was totaly unprepared last week when the great love of my young life, Gloria DeHaven, still exciting and glamorous at 53, strode into the office.

I stared like a schoolboy while she swept past my desk and into a conference room where she was to be interviewed by another member of the staff.

She sat in my line of vision, not more than 30 feet away, about the same distance as the front row seat from the screen at the Strand.

I watched the entire interview and when it was over she walked by me again, headed for the door. I had planned to speak to her, but she seemed in a hurry and I didn't want to interrupt.

A distinguished appearing gentleman who was accompanying her looked friendly. So, when he approached my desk, I said, "She's walking out of my life again and I'm still sitting here holding an empty popcorn bag."

He caught up to Miss DeHaven and repeated my comment.

She turned and looked at me and she smiled and said, "We have to stop meeting like this." Then she waved — and she was gone.

Part of me turned back to my desk and to the tasks at hand, but in my heart it was 3 a.m. and I was tap dancing down Broadway in the rain. An Irish cop, who looked strangely like Pat O'Brien, tipped his cap and smiled at me.

"Top o' the mornin' to you, officer," I said, under by breath.

Life, sometimes, is almost like the movies.